Edoardo Weiss

Also by Paul Roazen

Freud: Political and Social Thought (1968, 1986, 1999)

Brother Animal: The Story of Freud and Tausk (1969, 1990)

Freud and His Followers (1975)

Erik H. Erikson: The Power and Limits of a Vision (1976)

Helene Deutsch: A Psychoanalyst's Life (1985, 1992)

Encountering Freud: The Politics and Histories of Psychoanalysis (1990)

Meeting Freud's Family (1993)

How Freud Worked: First-Hand Accounts of Patients (1995)

Heresy: Sandor Rado and the Psychoanalytic Movement
(with Bluma Swerdloff) (1995)

Canada's King: An Essay in Political Psychology (1998)

Oedipus in Britain: Edward Glover and the Struggle Over Klein (2000)

Political Theory and the Psychology of the Unconscious (2000)

The Historiography of Psychoanalysis (2001)

The Trauma of Freud: Controversies in Psychoanalysis (2002)

Cultural Foundations of Political Psychology (2003)

On the Freud Watch: Public Memoirs (2003)

Edited by Paul Roazen

Sigmund Freud (1973)

Louis Hartz, *The Necessity of Choice:
Nineteenth Century Political Theory* (1990)

Helene Deutsch,
The Psychoanalysis of the Sexual Functions of Women (1991)

Victor Tausk, *Sexuality, War, and Schizophrenia:
Collected Psychoanalytic Papers* (1991)

Helene Deutsch, *The Therapeutic Process, the Self,
and Female Psychology: Collected Psychoanalytic Papers* (1991)

Paul Roazen

Edoardo Weiss

The House that Freud Built

Transaction Publishers
New Brunswick (U.S.A.) and London (U.K.)

This book is printed on acid-free paper that meets the American National Standard for Permanence of Paper for Printed Library Materials.

Library of Congress Catalog Number: 2004058073
ISBN: 0-7658-0270-8
Printed in the United States of America

Library of Congress Cataloging-in-Publication Data

Roazen, Paul, 1936-
Edoardo Weiss: the house that Freud built / Paul Roazen.
p. cm.
Includes bibliographical references and index.
ISBN 0-7658-0270-8 (alk. paper)
1. Weiss, Edoardo, 1889- 2. Psychoanalysts—Italy—Biography.
3. Psychoanalysts—United States—Biography. I. Title.

BF109.W42R63 2004
150.19'52'092—dc22 2004058073
[B]

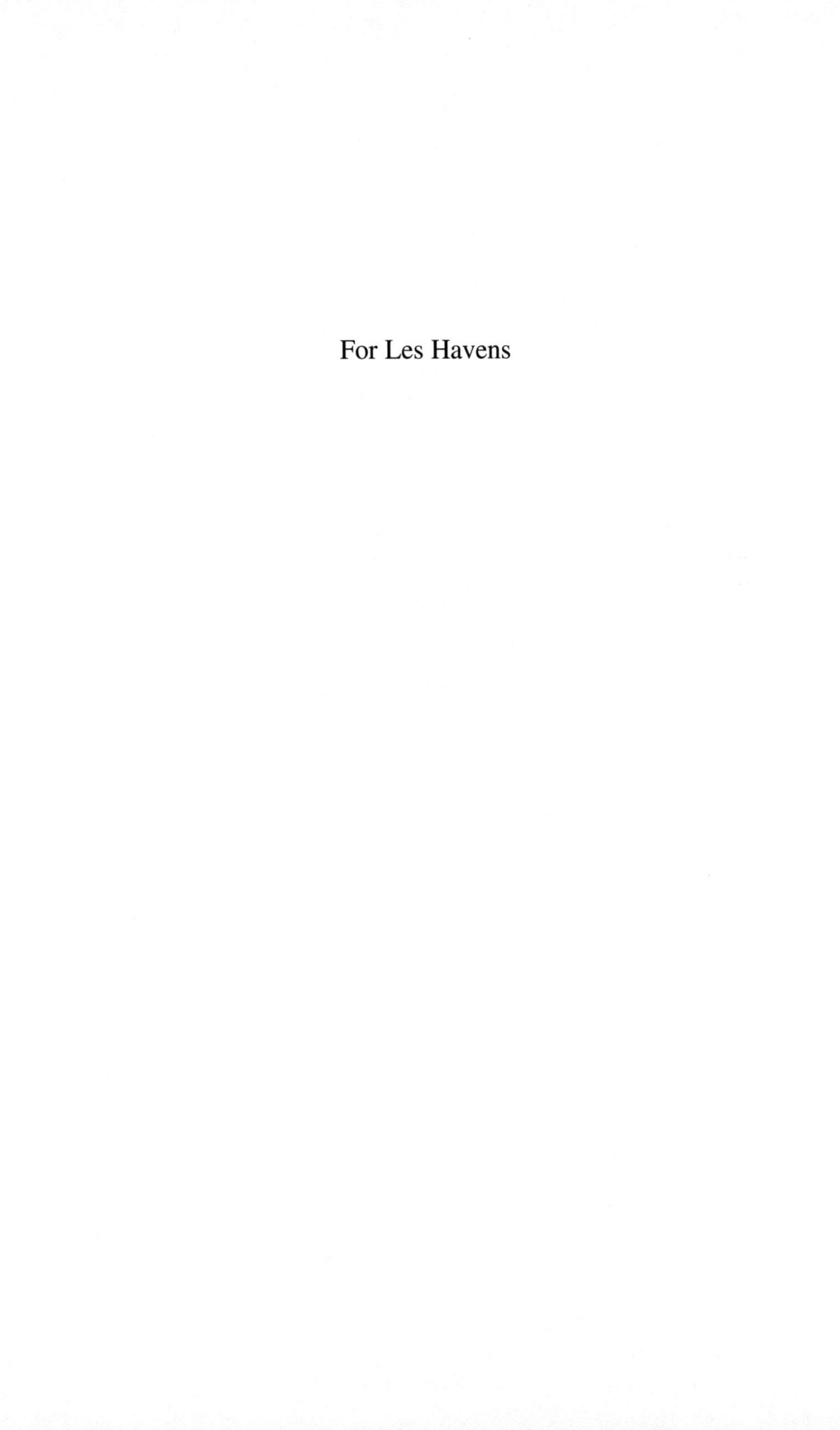

For Les Havens

Sweet are the uses of adversity,
Which, like the toad, ugly and venomous,
Wears yet a precious jewel in his head;
And this our life, exempt from public haunt,
Finds tongues in trees, books in the running brooks,
Sermons in stones, and good in everything:
I would not change it.

Duke Senior
As You Like It

Contents

Preface

This is a book that I have long been intending to write. In the course of my interviewing in the mid-1960s those who had known Sigmund Freud personally, I spent many hours, on twelve separate occasions, interviewing Dr. Edoardo Weiss (1889-1970) in Chicago. Although he is generally acknowledged as the founder of psychoanalysis in Italy, even now scarcely any literature about him exists.[1] The great literary scholar and James Joyce specialist Richard Ellmann did twice credit Weiss with having "introduced psychoanalysis into Italy" by 1910.[2] A small book of Freud's correspondence with Weiss appeared first in 1970, and Weiss and I had discussed together each of those precious primary documents before they came out in print.[3]

When, years later, I gave a lecture in Rome at the Italian Psychoanalytic Society (SPI) in 1995, it was then the larger of the two groups in Italy that were both members of the International Psychoanalytic Association (IPA), an organization first created at Freud's behest in 1910; that one Italian Psychoanalytic Society, known colloquially among local analysts by its street address as "Via Panama," now numbers, including members and candidates, approximately 1,000 people. At a time when psychoanalysis in America, for example, has been under a professional cloud, elsewhere in the world, as in Italy, where Freud's teachings have been more securely associated with philosophy and literature, psychoanalysts are doing much better. And so in Great Britain, France, Latin America, even Russia, Freud's school has continued notably to thrive. In places like India and China, Freudians and Jungians are today avidly competing for slicing up the impending psychotherapeutic pie as the traditional family systems get transformed along more individualistic Western lines. Psychoanalysis would seem to thrive on the spread of the modern notions of selfhood and personhood that it helped inspire.

In Rome, one could find in 1995 a large billboard advertising spectacles for sale by means of using an enlarged photograph of Freud's face in old age. The Italian psychoanalytic boom probably can be dated from the student radicalism of the late 1960s. Besides the dual Freudian groups in Italy, the Jungians have themselves been well enough established there to have long been split into two camps.[4] (As we shall see, Weiss had some personal involvement with an early leading Jungian in Rome.) One breakaway Jungian, Aldo Carotenuto, may be today the most popularly well-known contemporary exponent of any Italian branch of depth psychology. (The Freudians have had their own less well-known dissidents who have resigned, been marginalized, or even actively expelled.) In addition, Italy has traditionally had a special ear for Parisian developments, so recent followers of Jacques Lacan have also been active in a country whose Catholicism, prior to Weiss's own emigration to the States early in 1939, once made things especially difficult for this new profession and way of thinking. Other Italian forces, besides the Church, such as Benedetto Croce's idealism, Marxism, as well as positivistic psychiatry, seem also to have worked against the initial acceptance of Freud's teachings.

Although Italy has had no dominant psychoanalytic guru of its own, and therefore might appear to lack a separate native way of proceeding, the Italians, in keeping with their characteristic generosity and open-mindedness, have been exceptionally receptive to thinkers from other cultures. In addition to having brought out an unusually excellent scholarly edition of Freud (none exists even today in France), Italians have been translating Jung since 1903 and an impressive collected edition of his own works has also appeared there. An important "neo-Freudian" like Erich Fromm is still widely read in Italy. And I would guess that America's Harry Stack Sullivan is perhaps at least as well known now in Italy as in the States, since so many of his works are available in Italian. While Italians have been outgoing and pluralistic in their cosmopolitan receptivity to ideas that originated abroad, they have been wary of the mistake American analysts made in ignoring for too long psychopharmacological innovations; at the same time Italian therapists look on the American enthusiasm for the categories of DSM (Diagnostic and Statistical Manuals) with an appropriate degree of disdain and cultured incredulity.[5] A can-do approach to "solving" human dilemmas, when associated with the American-appearing myth of relying on the technologies of medication, cannot be expected easily to fit into Old World sensitivities about the endurance of the human condition. The greatest world literature has always assumed the inevitability of tragedy in a way that runs counter to how we are apt merely to trivialize the use of the word "tragedy" today.

When I first saw Edoardo Weiss at his office on April 5, 1965, I had just started interviewing Helene Deutsch in Cambridge, Massachusetts, where I then lived. My background was in the history of political and social philosophy, and my Ph.D. dissertation in political science had been on "Freud and Political Theory." The central educational direction I received as an undergraduate had been in the mid-1950s when Max Weber's thesis about the significance of the protestant ethic in matching the spirit of capitalism was treated as a notable effort to elevate the standing ideas could have in human action. It was a time when Marxian attitudes toward the alleged mere "superstructure" of intellectual history had little appeal for me. On the contrary, Lord Keynes had triumphantly succeeded in establishing the humanistic principle that how we think about economics can shape what policymakers actually do. And in this context Freud's work contributed to a hopeful conviction that our minds can singularly affect how we behave.

Even before I started seeing Weiss and Helene Deutsch, I had already met, in October 1964, Abram Kardiner in New York City, a leading pioneer in bringing together anthropology and psychoanalysis; and earlier I had interviewed in Boston the widow of the poet-psychiatrist Merrill Moore. Although Moore himself never got accepted as an analyst, these people had all once known each other, as would be the case with the approximately seventy early figures in psychoanalysis I eventually got to see. By the summer of 1965, I would be on my way, thanks to the recommendation Helene Deutsch offered, to Anna Freud and her clinic for children in Hampstead, London.

Right at the outset of my work on psychoanalysis in the early 1960s I had been especially interested in the comparative national reception of psychoanalytic ideas, although in those days I was initially only drawn to comparing and contrasting how Freud's work got received in England and America. By now, having traveled around the world and looked at events through the telescope of the impact of depth psychology in various different places, my knowledge has expanded on the subject of the possible varieties of cultural variations on common themes.

Weiss was personally frustrated at his efforts to introduce psychoanalysis in Italy, since because of the powerful opposition of the Catholic Church psychoanalytic books and publications had eventually started getting banned under Mussolini in 1934; but I will always remember Weiss as an unusually gentle and warm human being, at the same time serious-minded and determined. Today, when psychoanalysis is flourishing in Italy, Weiss has been formally honored as a pioneer. A nice avenue has been named for Weiss in his native Trieste, where a plaque has also been placed on a house where Weiss lived and practiced there. But although a drawing of him hangs in the auditorium at "Via Panama," I found in 1995 that almost no one present at my talk there knew much about Weiss's career or special contributions.

Although this study of his role and views, largely based on my interviews with him, is bound to seem informal, it may turn out to be the only biographical inquiry about him that will prove possible. He wrote six books and about a hundred professional papers, although in a style of thinking that did not successfully become established and therefore is bound to sound a bit alien to contemporary ears. It has been known that because of his therapeutic treatment in Rome of the daughter of one of Mussolini's cabinet ministers, a question has arisen about Freud's own relationship with the Italian dictator.[6] Furthermore, in Palermo Alessandra Tomasi di Palma, the wife of Giuseppe di Lampedusa—author of the great novel *The Leopard*—was a princess who also became an Italian analyst. To continue the relevance of psychoanalysis to twentieth century literature, both Weiss and Freud had in analysis Dr. Bruno Veneziani, a brother-in-law of Italo Svevo (born Ettore Schmitz) who wrote the outstanding *Confessions of Zeno* (1923).[7] Weiss had not only grown up in Svevo's Trieste, but was his nephew by marriage and a school-friend of his wife and brother-in-law. And a younger brother of Weiss's had married a niece of Svevo's. Early on Svevo (1861-1928) had read Freud and co-translated one of his books into Italian; literary critics have been tempted to think that the psychoanalyst, "Dr. S.," in Svevo's *Confessions* was probably modeled on Weiss.

In Trieste Weiss also analyzed in 1929-30 another famous writer of European reputation, Umberto Saba, who wrote novels, poetry, and books of non-fiction; Weiss said that Saba had "immediately" understood what psychoanalysis was about, and reacted most favorably. A student of Saba's work later described him as "a wholesale, doctrinaire convert to Freudian thinking."[8] Like Svevo, Saba (born Umberto Poli) had taken a pseudonym. Although Saba (1883-1957) had been dead for almost ten years when I met Weiss, he was still in correspondence with his daughter.[9] Decades after I met Weiss I discovered that Saba had dedicated a book of poems to him. Another important Italian poet, Sandro Penna, was also a patient of Weiss's.[10]

Weiss evidently was far less favorably inclined about Svevo's knowledge of psychoanalysis, in contrast to Saba's, and although Svevo had sent a copy of his *Confessions* directly to Freud the book went unacknowledged.[11] (We will be returning in chapter 7 to Freud's unfavorable attitudes toward Svevo's brother-in-law.) Freud's tastes in literature, and art, were rather old-fashioned, and just as one could not expect Freud to have appreciated the sarcasm about psychoanalysis from the great Viennese wit Karl Kraus, neither Weiss nor Freud could have readily appreciated how skeptically sophisticated about psychoanalysis someone like Svevo could be. Svevo was already the author of two remarkable, though unheralded novels, *A Life* (1893) and *Emilio's Carnival* (1898)[12], and in his *Confessions* Svevo was more or less taking for granted the import of what Freud had accomplished, while in practical terms Freud and Weiss were still mainly concerned with promoting "the cause" itself.

It was typical of Svevo's style of thinking that he later sounds rueful in commenting about his contact with Freud's psychoanalysis:

> It is the artist's destiny to be inspired by a philosopher whom he does not perfectly understand, and the philosopher's destiny not to understand the very artist he inspired…[The] intimate relationship between the artist and the philosopher is like that of a legal marriage, because like husband and wife they don't really understand each other and yet produce fine children...[13]

Svevo acknowledged of his *Confessions* that "there are two or three ideas in the novel which are actually taken entirely from Freud."

> [F]or a long time I thought I'd written a work of psychoanalysis. Now I have to say that when I published the book and looked forward to success, as anyone who publishes anything does, there was a deathly silence...Even a man with my experience of failure could not bear it: it took away my appetite and my sleep. At that time I ran into the only psychoanalytical doctor in Trieste, my good friend Dr. Weiss, and, nervously, he looked me in the eye and asked if he was the psychoanalyst in Trieste whom I made fun of in my novel.

Svevo claimed that it could not be Weiss because during World War I he was away doing military service: "Reassured, he accepted my book, which I had inscribed for him...." Weiss's younger son still today has that book, containing Svevo's dedication. Weiss had

> promised to study it, and to review it in a psychoanalytic journal in Vienna. For several days I slept and ate better. Success was at hand, because my work was going to be discussed in an internationally-known journal. However, when I saw him again, Dr. Weiss told me that he couldn't write about my book because it had nothing whatever to do with psychoanalysis.

Svevo reported having been "upset,"

> for it would have been a great thing if Freud had sent me a telegram saying: 'Thanks for having introduced psychoanalysis into Italian aesthetics'.... Now I am no longer upset. We novelists play games with the great philosophies without really being equipped to expand them. We falsify them, but we also humanize them. The superman, when he arrived in Italy, was not exactly Nietzsche's.[14]

Svevo may have been referring here to Mussolini. In any event, Svevo, who published his novels at his own expense, would only succeed in attaining a flourishing literary reputation largely after his death. When I met with Weiss, Svevo had not achieved the immortality he would seem to have attained today.

The old Trieste of Svevo and Weiss, when the city was still part of the Hapsburg Empire, was an immensely complicated part of the world; it had its own dialect, and Italian national aspirations to recapture that territory, the irredentism sometimes linked to fascism, had to play a special role in these people's lives. Weiss had served in the army of the Austro-Hungarian Empire in the First World War, while Italy itself entered on the side of the Allies in 1915. Svevo, who made his living working in his in-laws' business-firm, evidently wrote in a curiously almost "cumbersome" businessman's Italian.[15] Writers can be savage about each other: Saba said that "Svevo could write *well* in German; he preferred to write *badly* in Italian."[16] But Svevo's ironic and unusually subtle work (initially championed in the mid-1920s by Joyce in Paris) has succeeded in translating wonderfully well. Saba, in contrast, who made a project of mastering classic Tuscan literary Italian, remains far less known abroad.

It is partly because of the publications about the illustriousness of old Trieste's cultural achievements that I have been drawn back now to the material I once collected about Weiss's recollections; but he was in fact one of my key general early sources. For years now I have been trying to put into books what I once accumulated about the early days of psychoanalysis. And it is today mainly my historical conscience about Weiss that has bothered me. What would become of that which I long ago gathered but not yet put in print? It is this concern that has moved me now to publish what I found out. The present book can be considered a companion to my *Oedipus in Britain: Edward Glover and the Struggle Over Klein,*[17] even though there will be no comparable ideological controversy to match Glover's involvement with Melanie Klein's innovations in London. On the other hand, the immediacy of Weiss's involvement with Freud should have a special poignancy and historical significance all its own. He not only had numerous clinical consultations with Freud, but two of these cases were Weiss's sisters who were in analysis in Vienna with Freud.

The issue of lineage has been exceptionally important in many fields, and Freud himself was eager to call upon his own predecessors in the history of thought; his successors have continued to cite their origins within the family romance of the field he created.[18] People with the acknowledged public rank of Erik H. Erikson, and also Bruno Bettelheim, were both capable of inventing parts of their contact with Freud. (Erikson could later imagine that Freud came to the railroad station in Vienna to see Erikson's family off in 1933, despite Freud's advanced age and Erikson's lack of stature then; and at the end of his life Bettelheim claimed Freud had taken part in Bettelheim's supposedly being accepted for psychoanalytic training in Vienna just before the 1938 *Anschluss* with Hitler's Germany.[19]) Although Weiss never became a front-rank analytic thinker like either Erikson or Bettelheim, Weiss was the acknowledged leader of the movement in a country Freud cared about succeeding in. The genuine intimacy of Weiss's own contacts with Freud, plus the neglected story of his career, makes it worrisome to me that without this book he might be allowed to slip through the historical cracks. At the same time the story of his work, and the example of his unusual clinical kindliness and humanity, help to illustrate just how broad and rich the intellectual tradition initiated by Freud can be.

Notes

1. H. Stuart Hughes, *Prisoners of Hope: The Silver Age of the Italian Jews 1924-1974* (Cambridge, MA: Harvard University Press, 1983), p. 31, and "Obituary of Weiss," *New York Times*, Dec. 16, 1970. See also Ernst Federn, "Edoardo Weiss and the Beginnings of Psychoanalytic Ego Psychology," *Sigmund Freud House Bulletin*, Vol. 6, 1982, pp. 25-32, and Martin Grotjahn, *My Favorite Patient: The Memoirs of a Psychoanalyst* (Frankfurt: Peter Lang, 1987), pp. 152-53. Recently, Anna Maria Accerboni Pavanello has published a pamphlet about Weiss: *Trieste Nella Psicoanalisi* (Trieste: Editoriale Associati, 2002).
2. Richard Ellmann, *The Consciousness of Joyce* (New York: Oxford University Press, 1977), p. 54 and Richard Ellmann, *James Joyce*, revised edition (New York: Oxford University Press, 1983), p. 340. See also Ira B. Nadel, *Joyce and the Jews: Culture and Texts* (London: Macmillan, 1989).
3. Edoardo Weiss, *Sigmund Freud as a Consultant: Recollections of a Pioneer in Psychoanalysis*, with an introduction by Martin Grotjahn (New York: Intercontinental Medical Book Corporation, 1970). See a second, corrected edition of *Sigmund Freud as a Consultant*, with a new foreword by Emilio Weiss and a new Introduction by Paul Roazen (New Brunswick, NJ: Transaction Publishers, 1991).
4. Thomas B. Kirsch, *The Jungians: A Comparative and Historical Perspective* (London: Routledge, 2000; Philadelphia, PA: Taylor and Francis, 2000), pp. 147-155.
5. For surveys of psychoanalysis in Italy, see Michel David, *La psicoanalisi nella cultura italiana*, second edition (Turin: Bollati Boringhieri, 1990); Luigi Antonello Armando, *Storia della psicoanalisi in Italia dal 1971 al 1996* (Rome: Nuove Edizioni Romane, 1989). Also, Marco Conci, "Psychoanalysis in Italy: A Reappraisal," *International Forum of Psychoanalysis*, Vol. 3 (1994), pp. 117-26; Paolo Migone, "Psychoanalysis in Italy," *Academy Forum*, 1989, Vol. 33, 1-2, pp. 12-13, and 3-4, p. 3; 1990, Vol. 34, 3, p. 14; Sergio Benvenuto, "A Glimpse at Psychoanalysis in Italy," *Journal of European Psychoanalysis*, Number 5 (Spring-Fall 1997), pp. 33-50; Sergio Benvenuto, "On Italy," *Telos*, Nos. 98-99 (Winter 1993-

Spring 1994), pp. 217-28; and Arnaldo Novelletto, "Italy," in *Psychoanalysis International: A Guide to Psychoanalysis Throughout the World*, Vol. 1, ed. Peter Kutter (Stuttgart, Frommann-Holzboog, 1992), pp. 195-212.

6. See Paul Roazen, *The Trauma of Freud: Controversies in Psychoanalysis* (New Brunswick, NJ: Transaction Publishers, 2002), pp. 113-21. Also, see A. M. Accerboni, "Psychoanalysis and Fascism, Two Incompatible Approaches: The Difficult Role of Edoardo Weiss," *Review of the International History of Psychoanalysis*, Vol. 1 (1988), pp. 225-240; Glauco Carloni, "Freud and Mussolini: A Minor Drama in Two Acts, One Interlude, and Five Characters," *L'Italia nella Psicoanalisis*, *Italy in Psychoanalysis,* ed. Armaldo Novelletto (Rome, Enciclopedia Italiana, 1989), pp. 51-60; A. M. Accerboni Pavanello, "Sigmund Freud as Remembered by Edoardo Weiss, the Italian Pioneer of Psychoanalysis," *International Review of Psychoanalysis*, Vol. 18 (1990), pp. 351-59.
7. Italo Svevo, *Confessions of Zeno*, translated by Beryl de Zoete (New York: Vintage, 1989).
8. Umberto Saba, *Ernesto*, translated by Mark Thompson (London and New York: Carcanet, 1987), p. 149.
9. See Umberto Saba, *Lettere Sulla Psicoanalisi* (Milan, SE, 1991), pp. 89-92. See also Umberto Saba, *The Stories and Recollections of Umberto Saba*, translated by Estelle Gilson (Riverdale-on-Hudson, NY: 1993), Joseph Cary, *Three Modern Italian Poets: Saba, Ungaretti, Montale* (New York: New York University Press, 1969), and Anna Maria Pavanello Accerboni, "Il 'mito personale' di Umberto Saba: tra poesia e psicoanalisi," *Rivisita di Psicoanalisi*, vol. 30, no. 4 (Oct.-Dec. 1984), 546-59.
10. For this point I am indebted to Daniel Heller-Roazen.
11. P. N. Furbank, *Italo Svevo: The Man and the Writer* (London: Secker & Warburg, 1966), p. 177.
12. Italo Svevo, *A Life*, translated by Archibald Colquhoun (London: Pushkin Press, 2000), and Italo Svevo, *Emilio's Carnival*, translated by Beth Archer Brombert (New Haven, CT: Yale University Press, 2001).
13. Livia Veneziani Svevo, *Memoir of Italo Svevo*, translated by Isabel Quigley (Evanston, IL: The Marlboro Press/Northwestern University Press, 2001), pp. 99-100.
14. Ibid., pp. 97-98. See also Aaron Esman, "Italo Svevo and the First Psychoanalytic Novel," *International Journal of Psychoanalysis*, Vol. 82 (2001), pp. 1225-1233.
15. Joseph Cary, *A Ghost in Trieste* (Chicago: University of Chicago Press, 1993), p. 125.
16. Ibid., p. 152.
17. Paul Roazen, *Oedipus in Britain: Edward Glover and the Struggle Over Klein* (New York: Other Press, 2000).
18. Paul Roazen, "Charles Rycroft and the Theme of Ablation," *British Journal of Psychotherapy*, Vol. 18, No. 2 (2001), pp. 269-78. Also in Paul

Roazen, *On the Freud Watch: Public Memoirs* (London: Free Association Books, 2003), ch. 2, pp. 27-40.

19. Lawrence J. Friedman, *Identity's Architect: A Biography of Erik H. Erikson* (New York: Charles Scribner's Sons, 1999), p. 97 and Theron Raines, *Rising to the Light: A Portrait of Bruno Bettelheim* (New York: Alfred A. Knopf, 2002), pp. 489-90. See also Nina Sutton, *Bettelheim: A Life and a Legacy* (New York: Basic Books, 1996), p. 553 and Richard Pollak, *The Creation of Dr. B.: A Biography of Bruno Bettelheim* (New York: Simon and Schuster, 1997), p. 50.

1

Trieste

Weiss was born on September 21, 1889 in Trieste, a place that has increasingly stood out as one of the high-points in world cultural history.[1] It continues to attract scholarly attention, and has even been called "the greatest provincial capital of the twentieth century, a city that may not have equaled Paris or Berlin but certainly earned an extended chapter in the history of modernism."[2] Sons of Trieste like Svevo and Saba memorably lived and wrote their great works there. Joyce also knew Weiss's younger brother Ottocaro both in Trieste and Zurich,[3] although Weiss was altogether too modest to have stressed that connection to me. (Besides Saba, it turns out that Weiss also analyzed Roberto Bazlen [1902-65], a man of letters; Weiss was "on friendly terms with most of the small band of Triestine intellectuals and writers."[4]) Joyce had taught English at the Berlitz School in Trieste, and finished in that city his great book of short stories *Dubliners*. Joyce wrote not only *A Portrait of the Artist as a Young Man* in Trieste, but also parts of *Ulysses* in which at one point he played on the name "Weiss"[5]; *Finnegans Wake* had the famous line about "when they were yung and easily freudened." Gustav Mahler and Arturo Toscanini conducted in Trieste, and Rainer Maria Rilke was inspired by a castle outside the city to write his *Duino Elegies*. Franz Kafka worked for a Triestine insurance company in Prague, and Marcel Proust's narrator in his sequence of great novels was obsessed by the Trieste lesbian activities of "Albertine."

Situated at the extreme northeast corner of today's Italy, Trieste was originally a Roman garrison town, and later dominated by the Venetians during the twelfth and thirteenth centuries. In 1382 the city placed itself under the control of the Hapsburgs, who in turn created Trieste as a free port in 1719. The Austro-Hungarian Empire needed an outlet to the sea, and Trieste's location on the northern Adriatic made it the central access the Hapsburgs had to the advantages that water could bring for trade. In the last half of the eighteenth century the population increased from 6,433 in 1758 to between 20,000 and 24,000 around 1800. Not only was Trieste an accessible harbor for the Hapsburgs, Emperor Joseph II had also succeeded in transforming a small settlement into one of the great seaports in the world: "When Austria lost its north Italian provinces in 1859, Trieste became the empire's principal Mediterranean port."[6] In the late nineteenth century, Trieste was "the world's seventh busiest port, and second in the Mediterranean after Marseilles,"[7] ahead of both Genoa and Barcelona. Trieste's population jumped again over the course of the nineteenth century, and was "close to 180,000 at the start of the twentieth."[8] By 1910, the Triestine numbers, according to another authority, approached 220,000. We are told that "goods shipped to Europe from every continent were marked Via Trieste. The city came to be known as the 'third entrance to the Suez Canal' because so much traffic flowed from there to and from Asia."[9] Besides Trieste having five theatres, the 1909 presence of some twenty-one movie houses in Trieste prompted Joyce to try opening a movie theatre in Dublin, where it failed.

It was not just the Slavic and Italian that jostled together in Trieste, bordering what we now think of as the old Yugoslavia (in reality Slovenia), once run by Tito, but the Hapsburgs had succeeded in implementing in Trieste an unusual Enlightenment policy of religious toleration. Catholics, Orthodox Greeks, Protestants, and Jews were able to live together harmoniously; at the edge of the Balkans Trieste became "a cosmopolitan center that attracted diverse non-Catholic religious-ethnic minorities: Jews, Greek and Serbian orthodox, Protestants, and Armenians."[10] Around 1807 a French émigré aristocrat had written of Trieste to a merchant brother of his living there that "the past is dead": "The city you have chosen for your new undertakings is the most suitable and certain for your success; it is the Philadelphia of Europe, the city typical of pioneers of our old continent, the port where the shipwrecked find welcome and a promising new life."[11] Trieste could function that way thanks to Joseph II's 1781 Patent of Toleration so that non-Catholics, including Lutherans, Calvinists and the Greek orthodox, were given formal tolerance. In the context of these non-Catholic Christians, cultured Sephardic Jews were able to flourish there, since they were more worldly than their eastern brethren. Just to begin to indicate how complicated a linguistic world it was, under the Hapsburgs the official language was Italian, spoken by most—even for business that could get carried on in German. "Most educated Triestines were trilingual"[12]—in German, Slovene, and the Triestine dialect. So Trieste was capable of becoming a unique European refuge. Freud went there himself from Vienna in order to pursue neurological research in 1876.

Although by 1900 Trieste was the third largest city, following Vienna and Prague, in the Hapsburg Empire, the outbreak of World War I in 1914 proved Trieste's undoing, as well as the Hapsburgs with their 600-year-old Empire. After a Bosnian Serb in Sarajevo assassinated the Archduke Franz Ferdinand and his wife, their bodies were brought to Trieste by an Austro-Hungarian battleship. A funeral cortege through Trieste can be taken as the beginning of the end of the golden era of Trieste; aside from the illustriousness of its literature, no "great art galleries, museums, or monuments"[13] would be left behind. With the break-up of the Austro-Hungarian Empire at the end of World War I, Trieste lost its main *raison d'être* as a port and entered on a period of comparative decay. Although Trieste would become "a rich prize" when annexed to Italy, "it was not such an unqualified advantage for Trieste itself, since a political frontier now severed the Triestini from their German and Slav hinterland, leaving the city a head without a body and its inhabitants often without occupation." The loss of natural trade routes led to Trieste's decline.[14]

New countries were now carved out of the different nationalities of the old Hapsburg Empire—Hungary for example shrank to a fraction of its old size, and Vienna, instead of being the great imperial city, became a provincial capital of a small country known afterwards as Austria. Trieste (about a hundred miles to the east of Venice) first became part of the kingdom of Italy in 1918, and while remaining a free port was of no special strategic value, occupied in World War II by first the Nazis and then the Yugoslavs, until it finally was formally transferred to Italy in 1954. After the First World War Trieste became "a ghost of her pre-war self, commercially speaking…the Italian government had no intention of encouraging her at the expense of Venice."[15] Today Trieste, a secondary Italian port, is merely twice the size of New Haven, Connecticut.

Despite all its reduced standing starting after World War I, Trieste continues to symbolize a miraculous cultural era, one in which the Jews of Trieste, thanks to the existence of Greek merchants, were both able to help soften the power of the Catholic Church. Those exceptional years of Trieste's flourishing still stand as one of those precious moments in history where assimilated Jews (like Svevo and Saba) inhabiting this commercial city had a precarious opportunity to contribute to the free life of the mind. In the pre-World War I period the Jewish Triestine population amounted to about 6,000 people, or approximately 4 percent of the total, who — loyal to the Hapsburgs — enjoyed a rather favored standing compared to elsewhere in the Empire. For Trieste, "which prided itself on its relatively independent status, was, unlike Austria, where anti-Semitism ran rampant, a city where Jews had known early emancipation, were respected, and enjoyed a leading role in the community."[16] (Trieste was then about a tenth of the size of Vienna's two million, of which about 9 percent were Jewish.)

Weiss's father, Ignazio (1859-1936), was a successful Jewish businessman who was born in Bohemia, in a town about a hundred miles from Vienna. He had first come to Trieste in his twenties, and became an "industrialist" with a factory, producing eating oil, that employed four hundred people. Edoardo's mother, Fortuna (1867-1940), was, in contrast to her husband, a Jewish Italian of Sephardic origin, and a native of Trieste. Edoardo was the third child, the second son, of his parents' eight children. Although Edoardo's father was not lucky in getting a professional education, he was eager for his children to get higher training; two of Eduardo's brothers got their Ph.D.'s, the oldest one in physics and the younger one in economics.

Weiss's father also had belonged to the same B'nai B'rith lodge as Freud himself did, although the two men never met since Weiss's family remained in Trieste; in Europe B'nai B'rith was a highly selective cultural organization, not necessarily religious, and Freud had sometimes brought a paper of his there to read. Edoardo emphasized how in the Old World B'nai B'rith was almost a secret society, unlike what later became the case in America.

Edoardo was raised in a multi-lingual family; at the age of six his governess, for example, spoke in German. From his "early years" Edoardo Weiss said he was interested in the natural sciences, and while still attending the *gymnasium* (classical high school) getting an education he made the decision to study medicine, already with an eye on eventually becoming a psychiatrist. He first read Freud's *The Interpretation of Dreams* in 1905-1907; the bookseller in a mix-up ordered instead of the dream book Freud's relatively minor "Delusions and Dreams in Jensen's *Gradiva*," about a novella by Wilhelm Jensen, but both texts made an enduring impression on him. (Freud's *Gradiva* study was partly written to please Jung.) Weiss read both works before going to Vienna to study in 1908; he enrolled in the medical school of the University of Vienna, then still a natural center of cultural life for someone from Trieste, which did not yet have a university of its own. Weiss was already interested in psychology, and thought it would be a good idea to have an analysis. He had decided to study psychiatry before meeting Freud.

Although Weiss was fully aware of the hostility among the leading Viennese professors towards Freud's teachings, in early October 1908 he visited Freud, then fifty-two years old, to ask for his advice about how Weiss could be trained in psychoanalysis. Freud had started assembling his own circle of followers in 1902. During that 1908 interview Freud inquired about Weiss's background and personal life; Freud had asked the young man "whether he was satisfied with himself," and Freud then inquired into the nature of the "personal troubles" that he had. Weiss implied that there was nothing very striking here, and that his own difficulties were within the range of what could be expected. Evidently Weiss was shy, "bashful," and mainly had youthful "inhibitions" and some "obsessive" symptoms.

At that time Freud was already beginning to advise anyone intending to become an analyst to undergo personal analysis, a suggested approach that Freud once acknowledged Jung had introduced into the field.[17] Freud had been specific that "if Weiss got analyzed" he "could analyze others" afterwards. Even though it was already a hope of Freud's for the future that all analysts be analyzed, many unanticipated problems connected with such a proposal would crop up in the future. Freud never wanted to lose personal control over his movement, and was loath to see his profession become bound by bureaucratic rules. In the end it was only after Freud got cancer of the jaw in 1923 that he was forced to accept the inevitability of institutionalizing his own charisma, and the idea about training analyses for all future analysts became a formal requirement at an international IPA Congress in 1925.

Weiss, who had only just turned nineteen by the fall of 1908 and was an entering medical student, would take six years to complete becoming a doctor. Now Freud had not himself been analyzed, but neither had many of his earliest supporters either. (Jung had some personal treatment in Zurich.) Freud chose as the most appropriate analyst for Weiss the Viennese internist Paul Federn (1871-1950), who had first joined Freud's circle in 1903, and was therefore among Freud's oldest adherents.[18] Federn, although never analyzed himself, became one of the notable teachers in the history of psychoanalysis. He was a prominent old-time apostle of Freud's, and I knew that in 1952 Weiss had, in accordance with Federn's will, edited a volume of Federn's papers, *Ego Psychology and the Psychoses*.[19] Many leading analysts were to be trained by Federn, before and after his moving to New York City at the outset of World War II. Federn's students included many illustrious professional names: August Aichhorn, Edward Bibring, Otto Fenichel, Smith Ely Jelliffe, Heinrich Meng, Angel Garma, Alfhild Tamm, and Wilhelm Reich. The poet Rilke came to Federn for a brief period, as did the novelist Hermann Broch. It took me awhile to appreciate the full emotional role that Federn came to play in Weiss's life.

Freud had written Weiss's name on the top of one of Freud's calling cards, then Federn's name, and next put two Greek letters as a symbol of psychoanalysis. (The only aspect of my own poor education that genuinely shocked Weiss was my ignorance of ancient Greek.) The meetings of analysts in Vienna still had a secret atmosphere, and the Viennese in general thought ill of analysis. A famous Viennese neurologist, Lother Frankl von Hochwart,[20] would later once back Weiss up against a wall about a case of hysteria which, Frankl-Hochwart mockingly whispered, Weiss as an analyst would explain by her having once watched her grandmother urinating. However cynical he might sound, Frankl-Hochwart was reported to have been a bachelor who was immensely cultured and had elegant manners, with a disease of the peripheral nervous system named for him. All the early analysts were full of stories of the characteristic misunderstandings of Freud: Otto Marburg, another Viennese neurologist, had once pronounced to Weiss: "After Casanova comes Freud."

Weiss's association with Federn proved to be a decisive influence and of the greatest significance for his life as an analyst. Weiss's analysis with Federn, begun on March 1, 1909, developed into a lifelong friendship. Weiss was elected a member of the Vienna Psychoanalytic Society in 1913, and retained that status even after having moved to Rome in 1931, where he finally succeeded in founding the Italian Psychoanalytic Society in 1932.

At the end of Weiss's 1908 initial interview with Freud, when he was about to leave Freud's office, Weiss inquired how much money he owed Freud for the consultation, but Freud charmingly refused any payment on the grounds, as he told the young nineteen-year-old boy, that a "colleague" did not pay anything. Throughout the rest of Freud's life, starting from that first meeting in 1908, Weiss stayed continually in personal contact with him until his death in London in 1939.

Notes

1. Joseph Cary, *A Ghost in Trieste* (Chicago: University of Chicago Press, 1993); Claudio Magris, *Microcosms*, translated by Iain Halliday (London: Harvill Press, 1999); Lois C. Dubin, *The Port Jews of Habsburg Trieste* (Stanford, CA: Stanford University Press, 1999).
2. Nicholas Howe, "Triste Trieste," *New Republic*, Sept. 2, 2002, pp. 31-37.
3. Richard Ellmann, *James Joyce*, revised edition (New York: Oxford University Press, 1983), pp. 393-94, 396, 398, 451, 455, 460, 462-64, 467, 473.
4. Cary, *A Ghost in Trieste*, p. 228.
5. Corinna del Greco Lobner, *James Joyce's Italian Connection: The Poetics of the Word* (Iowa City: University of Iowa Press, 1989), p. 102.
6. Saba, *Ernesto* (London and New York: Carcanet, 1987) p. 154; Furbank, *Italo Svevo*: *The Man and the Writer* (London: Secker and Warburg, 1966), p. 16.
7. John Banville, "Joyce in Bloom," *New York Review of Books*, Feb. 8, 2001, p. 37.
8. Cary, *A Ghost in Trieste*, p. 112.
9. Howe, op. cit., p. 32.
10. Dubin, *The Port Jews of Habsburg Trieste*, p. 1.
11. Howe, "Triste Trieste," p. 34.

12. Elizabeth Mahler-Schächter, "Svevo, Trieste, and the Vienna Circle: Zeno's Analyst Analysed," *European Studies Review*, vol. 12, no. 1 (Jan. 1982), p. 45.
13. Tim Parks, "Worth a Detour," *New York Review of Books*, March 24, 1994, p. 30.
14. Denis Mack Smith, *Modern Italy: A Political History* (Ann Arbor: University of Michigan Press, 1997), pp. 278, 388.
15. Furbank, *Italo Svevo*, p. 146.
16. Victor Brombert, "Svevo's Witness," *American Scholar* (Summer 1991), p. 426.
17. Paul Roazen, "The Problem of Silence: Training Analyses," *International Forum of Psychoanalysis*, Vol. 11 (2002), pp. 73-77. See also Roazen, *On the Freud Watch: Public Memoirs* (London: Free Association Books, 2003), ch. 4, pp. 51-57.
18. Martin S. Bergmann, "The Place of Paul Federn's Ego Psychology in Psychoanalytic Metapsychology," *Journal of the American Psychoanalytic Association*, Vol. 11, No. 1 (Jan. 1963), pp. 97-116; Edoardo Weiss, "Paul Federn: The Theory of the Psychosis," in *Psychoanalytic Pioneers*, ed. by Franz Alexander, Samuel Eisenstein, and Martin Grotjahn (New York: Basic Books, 1966), pp. 142-59; Ernst Federn, "Thirty-Five Years with Freud: In Honour of the 100th Anniversary of Paul Federn," *Journal of Clinical Psychology*, Monograph Supplement No. 32 (January 1972); Roazen, *Freud and His Followers* (New York: Alfred A. Knopf, 1975; New York: Da Capo, 1992), pp. 304-310.
19. Paul Federn, *Ego Psychology and the Psychoses*, edited and with an introduction by Edoardo Weiss (New York: Basic Books, 1952).
20. Roazen, *Helene Deutsch: A Psychoanalyst's Life* (New Brunswick, NJ: Transaction Publishers, 1992), pp. 121-22.

2

Chicago

When I first met Weiss he had been in Chicago for almost thirty years. He had initially gone from Italy in 1939 to the Menninger Clinic in Topeka, Kansas, then already affiliated with the Chicago Psychoanalytic Society. In Topeka, Weiss has been described as having been relatively "reclusive," and not particularly "popular."[1] We need to recall how powerful and long-lasting psychoanalytic orthodoxy on proper "technique" could be. According to the leading historian of the Menningers, "several American staff within the Topeka Psychoanalytic Institute had accused Edoardo Weiss of treating his analytic patients in sitting postures and seeing them only three times a week 'in conformity to his wife's thinly disguised Jungian approach.'"[2] Looking over the short membership lists in those days, this judgment can have reflected the views of a tiny number of people. Still, it would indeed have been considered an accusation then if Weiss did not always use the analytic couch for patients, and four or five sessions a week would have been considered a more standard frequency. Of course any hint of a "Jungian approach," even on the part of Weiss's wife Wanda, would have seemed like treason. Evidently Karl Menninger in particular had "fascination but scorn for Weiss's Jungian 'spiritualism and mysticism.'"[3]

Franz Alexander (1891-1964), who had once been the Hungarian-born prodigy of the Berlin Psychoanalytic Society's Training Institute, became the central figure who created psychoanalysis in Chicago and a key contact Weiss relied on to get him established in the New World. Unlike the way Helene Deutsch and Alexander both arrived in the States, each of them accompanied by an entourage of analytic patients, many of them American, Weiss had had to leave behind in Rome the three or four Italian candidates in training he had had then. Although when I first saw Weiss I technically knew of his early association with Trieste, in my American mind then he was mainly closely associated with Italy (meaning Rome) and Chicago.

I had myself spent my first year of graduate work at the University of Chicago in 1958-59, and it was at a wedding of a classmate and close friend of mine there in the early 1960s that I happened to meet a famous Chicago psychoanalyst, Gerhart Piers. I already had lots of questions about the explanations for what then seemed like the notable success of psychoanalysis in America, and in turn I was referred by Piers for my questions to the younger analyst Heinz Kohut. It is unlikely that at the time I even knew that Kohut was himself from Vienna, but I remember we had a nice luncheon together, and Kohut also took me to his office where he sent me off with a few interesting reprints, on music and Thomas Mann, of his own. Although I found Kohut agreeable and a cultured European, it never dawned on me that he would later become a leader of a movement that became known as "self-psychology."[4]

I first saw Weiss himself in Chicago almost entirely because I knew there had been letters from Freud to Weiss. At that time the then recent collection *Letters of Sigmund Freud*[5], edited by his son Ernst, was one of the main primary documentary sources in existence on my subject. Although I had not yet discovered how tendentiously that volume had been put together, passages being cut out without even any indication, by means of proper ellipses, that such omissions had been made, the list of addresses in the book, identifying Freud's correspondents, was an invaluable clue to a number of people still living who could be reliable informants about what Freud had been like. And a further tip-off to my quest for interviewing information was that in Volume III of Ernest Jones's official biography of Freud, Jones had, in an appendix consisting of thirty-eight extracts from Freud's correspondence, quoted fragments from three letters to Weiss.[6] It turned out that Weiss had had a large packet of letters from Freud to him, mainly about clinical issues, which only came out as that separate volume in 1970, the year Weiss died. (We will come back later to the special reasons Freud's daughter Anna had for minimizing the significance of this correspondence.)

When I met him Weiss had been in Chicago since 1940; although by now Alexander's name has virtually disappeared from public memory, at the time it was not hard accurately to suppose that he had been the main channel by which Weiss landed in America. It bears repeating that Topeka's small psychoanalytic group had originally been connected with Alexander's Chicago Psychoanalytic Society. Karl Menninger was analyzed by, among others, Alexander, and he and his brother Will were notably receptive to helping rescue other psychoanalytic and psychiatric refugees from European fascism. Alexander had been the inspiring leader of Chicago's analysts since becoming the first visiting professor of psychoanalysis at the University of Chicago in 1930. Alexander was widely considered a brilliant and original thinker, and Freud's middle son Oliver was only one of many in an elite to have been in analysis with him in Berlin[7]; at the time Alexander left for America Freud had been sorry (and angry) to lose him from Europe.

Alexander, whose father had been a philosopher in Budapest, was seriously interested in the history of psychiatry, and did much to help forward the subject; but he also deserves to be known for having been innovative in therapeutic technique, as well for specializing in psychosomatic medicine. Some of Alexander's therapeutic proposals were at the time considered heretically new; he thought that to hope for change from interpretive insight alone was too rationalistic, and psychoanalysts were encouraged to offer patients a "corrective emotional experience" as well.[8] For years Alexander, along with his fellow Hungarian Sandor Rado, would be considered by many to be in the family doghouse because of their liberalism. [9] However dubious to leaders of the reigning orthodoxy Alexander might have appeared to have been, right up until 1956, when he abruptly left to head a psychiatric department in Los Angeles, he had succeeded in breathing life into the Chicago Psychoanalytic Institute. Weiss indicated to me that although he had himself "disagreed" with Alexander on many points, Weiss still thought of him as "a good friend."

When I visited Chicago in 1965 it was still true that though Alexander, who had died the year before, was long gone from the local scene, it was quietly being suggested that he had been a more "controversial" leader than those who wanted to be organizationally acceptable elsewhere might have wanted to remember. (Although the "problem" that would later arise with Heinz Kohut's new "self-psychology" was still several years on the horizon for Chicago analysts, it still remains true today that accounts of that Institute's history, and the milieu for Kohut's early work, are apt to neglect the apparently dread name of Alexander. The same concern about the legitimacy of their lineage would also be characteristic of Washington, D.C. analysts, although there the local creative leader in need of being lived down for the sake of organizational conformity was Harry Stack Sullivan.) Yet Alexander had succeeded in creating at the Chicago Institute more of a genuine research orientation than any other analytic center I ever came across. Many analysts then had their offices on the same floor of a downtown building, and they therefore could easily meet for working luncheon discussions; Alexander had tried to make the group approximate standards that would be appropriate in normal university life.

Weiss, however, seemed pretty much an outsider in 1965. (From 1959 to 1961 he had been visiting professor in the Department of Psychiatry at Marquette University in Milwaukee.) He was widely regarded professionally as dependable and reliable, quiet and soft-spoken, more low-key and less of a prima donna than other European analysts. He was also perhaps looked down as rather old-fashioned and not up-to-date psychoanalytically. As I was to find with Edward Glover in Britain, an analyst's marginal position can be a special source of insight. Coming from Trieste, Weiss would know the benefits as well as difficulties associated with marginality; Ernest Jones in Britain, Marie Bonaparte in Paris, and Freud in Vienna had all been in their different ways outsiders. Original people pay penalties for their nonconformity.

Weiss was considered loyal to his patients, and faithful in following up on them. When he had first come to Chicago in 1940, the pioneering American analyst in the city, Lionel Blitzstein, had been deferential to Weiss at Blitzstein's seminars. As time went on, various analysts, like Theresa Benedek, Maxwell Gitelson, as well as Weiss, would hold small meetings every few weeks with their own groups. In a sense then, separate sects existed within the one psychoanalytic institute, although I subsequently wondered how adept Weiss could have been in navigating within the Byzantine politics of his profession.

Weiss told me with a rather bitter chuckle how he had recently been made a staff member "emeritus" at the Chicago Institute. I could not then figure out whether the problem he had had was due to his age (he was by then seventy five), or also his prior friendly association with Alexander. The quiet warmth of Weiss's smile, as for example he looked at an old caricature of Alexander that I showed him, was unforgettable. Besides such drawings, I always found photographs an excellent way of stimulating memories and reflections.

As a European, Weiss naturally brought a different perspective than his American-born colleagues. But other continentals managed to flourish there, and part of the difficulty may have precisely been Weiss's secure personal association with Freud. Weiss's allegiance to Federn's less than fashionable, almost esoteric, ideas also was a source of Weiss's relative isolation; Weiss expressed some annoyance at how Kohut could ignore Federn, who pioneered in writing on the self, and that someone like Erik H. Erikson, so concerned with the concept of identity, failed to keep up with Federn personally. A man like Weiss was not about to run with the foxes or hunt with the hounds; he did not need to try to absorb the latest in fashionable thinking, seemed to me notable in failing to assign his own writings at seminars, and stuck to his guns about the reliability of his own experience.

When I knew him Weiss seemed a relatively short (5' 9"), kindly rather lonely man who had first-hand memories to report about Freud, whose unpublished letters to him Weiss cherished as historical documents. Weiss had a small office on the top floor of a building, separate from where the Psychoanalytic Institute itself was located, in a fairly expensive part of town. I can never forget how I had been tempted to leave on a table in the waiting room my copy of the morning *New York Times* I had finished reading, but Weiss clearly indicated that that would be improper (presumably a disturbance) for patients who came later; as a clinician Weiss was sensitive to the need his clients had for the emotional constancy of their surroundings. When I later came to interview him also at his apartment on the south side of Chicago, near the University where I had once done graduate work, I learned how modestly he lived. Weiss still had a busy practice, but compared to others I saw, who lived for example in large and expensive homes on the east side of New York City, Fifth and Park Avenues for example, he had scarcely the recognition that one might have expected his position to have earned. He nonetheless said he was "very glad" to be in America rather than Italy; more was doing then psychoanalytically, he remarked, in Buenos Aires than in Rome.

Only years later did I discover that Weiss's office furniture had been designed by Freud's architect son Ernst. (In New York, Sandor Rado had at least indicated to me that that same Freud son had constructed his office equipment.)

It was not long in my early interviews with Weiss before I got the message that I was taking up a lot of his time. Here I think that when I returned to Chicago, with my agenda of seeing him as well as other early analysts, my multiple interviews had the unintended consequence of succeeding in persuading Weiss of the legitimacy of my efforts. At least one key American-born analyst in Chicago, a power then at the Psychoanalytic Institute, informed Weiss of the importance of my inquiries, and I think that Weiss's felt need to appease such an inside authority meant I succeeded with Weiss partly by inadvertence.

In any event Weiss made a virtue out of what appeared to be a necessity, and he soon came up with the idea that I should write a biographical sketch of him to satisfy the request of analysts back in Italy. It was not hard for me to perform the requested chore. But for me every time I was in Weiss's presence I learned something new, and only partly in response to the kind of questions I came to ask. In his office, for example, there was a color picture of Federn on a wall, as well as a photograph of Freud in old age; I could not help noticing a copy of the famous 1914 Max Pollack etching of Freud, staring over his desk filled with Greek antiquities. And Weiss also had a small sculpture of Freud on a side-table, as well as a bust of Federn elsewhere in the office. A large European glass-fronted set of cabinets and bookcases was prominent, and from it Weiss was apt to pull items for me to read. He himself used a magnifying glass to study on a six-foot mahogany desk from Italy what he wanted to look at. Although before I set out to meet Weiss I had read some of his books, there was much about his work he needed to teach me.

What I learned came partly from the atmospherics of being with him. When he first happened to use the word "neurologist," it sounded to me exactly the same way Freud spoke in English on a recording of his voice made in London before his death.[10] Right from the outset I was inclined to ask questions about Freud's attitude toward Italy; apparently Freud had not thought too well of the Italian national character, as it was characteristic of the Viennese to look down on Italians, but when it came to art, sculpture and literature Weiss maintained that Freud was fully appreciative of what Italy had contributed. After the breakthrough of Freud's first trip to Rome in 1901, since he had needed to overcome an earlier inhibition, Italy became one of Freud's favorite holiday destinations. Giuseppe Garibaldi had played a role in Freud's own family romance, since Freud commented in his *The Interpretation of Dreams* "how like Garibaldi" Freud's own father had looked on his deathbed.[11] In the course of Garibaldi's fight against the Vatican City, the anti-clerical Masonic movement had many Jews in it.

If I had been adequately aware of Weiss's background in old Trieste I would have appreciated how Weiss could hold himself distant from developments in Italy. Weiss had analyzed in Rome two of the early Italian analysts, Emilio Servadio and Nicola Perrotti, both of whom got elected to membership with Weiss in the Vienna Psychoanalytic Society. Weiss was proud that before he had founded the Italian Psychoanalytic Society these pupils of his had been so accepted by Freud. Early on Weiss had offered to show me Freud's fifty letters to him, discussing over twenty-five cases; my own shyness in picking up on his offer was initially disappointing to him. But however my own lack of experience with such interviewing might have hindered how I proceeded, Weiss did keep agreeing to see me.

Notes

1. Lawrence J. Friedman, *Menninger: The Family and the Clinic* (New York: Alfred A. Knopf, 1990), p. 114.
2. Ibid., p. 120.
3. Ibid., p. 385.
4. Charles B. Strozier, *Heinz Kohut: The Making of a Psychoanalyst* (New York: Farrar, Straus and Giroux, 2002); Paul Roazen, *Encountering Freud: The Politics and Histories of Psychoanalysis* (New Brunswick, NJ: Transaction Publishers, 1990), pp. 221-23; Paul Roazen, *The Historiography of Psychoanalysis* (New Brunswick, NJ: Transaction Publishers, 2001), pp. 141-43; Paul Roazen, *Cultural Foundations of Political Psychology* (New Brunswick, NJ: Transaction Publishers, 2003), pp. 118, 176-177. See also Douglas Kirsner, *Unfree Associations: Inside Psychoanalytic Institutes* (London: Process Press, 2000), ch. 3, pp. 108-38.
5. *Letters of Sigmund Freud, 1873-1939*, edited by Ernst L. Freud, translated by Tania and James Stern (London: The Hogarth Press, 1961).
6. Ernest Jones, *The Life and Work of Sigmund Freud*, vol. 3: *The Last Phase* (New York: Basic Books, 1957), pp. 453-56.
7. Paul Roazen, *Meeting Freud's Family* (Amherst: University of Massachusetts Press, 1993), chs. 11-12.
8. See Franz Alexander and Thomas M. French with Catherine Lillie Bacon, *Psychoanalytic Therapy* (New York: The Ronald Press, 1946); *Dynamic Psychiatry*, ed. Franz Alexander and Helen Ross (Chicago: University of Chicago Press, 1952); Franz Alexander, *Psychoanalysis and Psychotherapy* (New York: W. W. Norton, 1956). For a critical assessment of Alexander's contribution, see Kurt R. Eissler, "The Chicago Institute of Psychoanalysis and the Sixth Period of the Development of Psychoanalytic Technique," *Journal of General Psychology*, vol. 42, First Half (January 1950), pp. 103-57. Also, see "Recollections of Franz Alexander," Interviews with Kurt Eissler (Library of Congress), Leon J. Saul, "Franz Alexander," *Psychoanalytic Quarterly*, vol. 33 (1964), pp. 420-23, and Martin Grotjahn, "Franz Alexander: The Western Mind in Transition," Alexander, Eisenstein, and Grotjahn (eds.), *Psychoanalytic Pioneers*, pp. 384-98.
9. See Franz Alexander, "Sandor Rado: The Adaptational Theory," in *Psychoanalytic Pioneers*, ed. by Alexander, Eisenstein, and Grotjahn, pp. 240-48; Paul Roazen and Bluma Swerdloff, *Heresy: Sandor Rado and the Psychoanalytic Movement* (Northvale, NJ: Jason Aronson, 1995); Paul Roazen, *The Trauma of Freud: Controversies in Psychoanalysis* (New Brunswick, NJ: Transaction Publishers, 2002), ch. 13, pp. 259-75.
10. *The Diary of Sigmund Freud 1929-1939: A Record of the Final Decade*, translated, annotated, with an introduction by Michael Molnar (New York: Charles Scribner's Sons, 1992), p. xxvi.

11. "The Interpretation of Dreams," *The Standard Edition of the Complete Psychological Works of Sigmund Freud*, translated and edited by James Strachey, vol. 5 (London: The Hogarth Press, 1953-74), pp. 447, 428. Hereafter this edition of Freud's works will be referred to simply as *Standard Edition*.

3

The Case of Frank

As I commented to myself in my first set of interview notes with Weiss, he "talked a blue-streak, I scarcely got a word in edge-wise." With Glover too in London I was struck by the contrast in what one might naively have expected of a normally silent analyst. And as I had also found interviewing Helene Deutsch, Weiss was fascinated by Freud's personality and character; in hindsight now I see that whereas she was in particular eager to talk about a former patient of hers, Victor Tausk, and how his difficulties with Freud shed light on the psychology of the creator of psychoanalysis, right from the outset with me Weiss pushed to the forefront how one of his patients, whom Weiss called "Frank," could illuminate Freud's own neurotic symptomatology. Even so, I was to be slow in picking up the full significance that "Frank" had for Weiss.

Psychoanalysis has now made us familiar with the idea that minor-seeming quirks of character can be exceptionally revealing about someone as a whole. Weiss had in Italy published a 1931 general book about psychoanalysis, which is still in print there today, to which Freud had written an introduction.[1] However brief Freud had been, that sort of endorsement had to be a special sign of Freud's special favor. Although the Berlin analyst Max Eitingon was in 1932 hesitant about admitting to the International Psychoanalytic Association the new Italian group Weiss had founded, Freud had written Eitingon: "The person of its leader is a sure guarantee as to the group's development, he alone is worth a group…."[2] (In 1914 Freud referred in print to his favorite in Budapest, Sandor Ferenczi: "Hungary, so near geographically to Austria, and so far from it scientifically, has produced only one collaborator, S. Ferenczi, but one that indeed outweighs a whole society."[3]) Weiss had also published in Italian a 1936 book on agoraphobia, the fear of open spaces; that year Freud said of the Italian movement that the "name Edoardo Weiss assures it a rich future."[4] Freud also once called Weiss a "true, tough pioneer"; and in writing to Arnold Zweig Freud referred to Weiss as "our brave colleague."[5] In corresponding with Ernest Jones, Freud had said Weiss was "a particularly good fellow and I should like to accommodate him as much as possible."[6]

In 1964 Weiss's latest book, *Agoraphobia in the Light of Ego Psychology*[7], had just come out. Whereas nowadays the term "panic attack" has become fashionable, agoraphobia was once the clinical term for talking about similar phenomena. Perhaps not surprisingly Weiss was exceptionally interested in pursuing with me the subject of agoraphobia (a topic on which Weiss knew that Helene Deutsch had also been memorably interested in). And so at my first encounter with Weiss he began talking with me by discussing, in the context of that patient Weiss had named "Frank," the issue of Freud's own agoraphobic problem, and what it could be taken to have meant about him in general.

Weiss brought to my attention that Theodor Reik had mentioned in print that once while walking with Freud in Vienna he had taken Reik's arm crossing a square, explaining that he still was afraid of a return of an old agoraphobic symptom he used to have.[8] In a newly published letter of Freud's he wrote in 1909 that "ambitious phantasies gone to ruin seem to be the specific factor in agoraphobia."[9] Weiss had a host of private hypotheses, none of which he ever published, to deal with this agoraphobic difficulty of Freud's; in particular Weiss wanted to explain it by means of a case of his own, that of "Frank," which Weiss had discussed at length in his most recent book.[10] (In the course of my subsequently seeing Weiss, I put my mind to reading all of his texts and technical papers; as I have already indicated, Weiss's ideas had been expressed in such a special framework as to be by 1965 off-the-beaten-track.) Whereas Reik had been straightforward in dealing with the subject of this particular neurotic symptom in Freud, Weiss only felt comfortable doing so by indirection. Yet Reik so revered Freud as to be more inhibited in trying to psychoanalyze his master.

Like Freud who had become fascinated with archeology, "Frank" had a special concern with classical antiquity, which he taught; and they both had fainting spells and exceptional death anxieties.[11] Weiss was also particularly concerned with the problem of "derealization," or feelings of unreality, which Frank too shared in having. (Evidently as a young man Weiss had himself also experienced such moods of estrangement; an Italian biographer of Weiss has concluded, on the basis of some youthful notebooks that Weiss kept, that "Frank" must have been Weiss himself.[12] But in his talks with me, Weiss mentioned in passing that he had been in contact with "Frank" in later years, whom Weiss referred to by an Italian first name, "Lorenzo." Thirty years after the treatment was over, Weiss thought that it was all right to publish the case, but not to translate it into Italian. I believe that "Frank" was a genuine case of Weiss's, who was fascinating to Weiss partly because of all the similarities Weiss found in him to Freud's own special kinds of problems. But one should not rule out any psychologist's use of his work to gain self-understanding.) "Frank" had, like Freud, a horror at the sight of blood, and both of them shared a memorable bedwetting incident in childhood.

Weiss was proud of having in late 1930 presented a paper on the subject of the role of the superego's guilt feelings in promoting reactions of unreality; this presentation was made at a small gathering of the Vienna analysts that met regularly then at Freud's home, in the spacious waiting room outside his office, at a time when Freud no longer was making public appearances. (Federn played a special role in helping to decide which analysts should attend these private meetings.) Weiss said that when he had arrived for the evening session he had been given the most cordial kind of welcome by Freud, as a father to a son who had returned after a long absence.

Weiss thought it noteworthy that before he began delivering his 1930 paper, Freud had taken him aside to indicate that Weiss should not take it personally if the group disagreed with what he had to say. To Weiss's surprise, therefore, it turned out that the analysts present, even those with a reputation for great orthodoxy, responded favorably to his ideas, and Freud had to admit at the end that perhaps he had been wrong in his prediction of trouble. To Weiss it seemed that only Freud might have differed from him. Then in 1936 Freud published a paper of his own on the subject called "A Disturbance of Memory on the Acropolis,"[13] dealing with a similar process of guilt-provoked disavowal; but Freud had not mentioned here Weiss's earlier essay. (Freud did say that his daughter Anna was preparing a book on the ego's methods of defense, but she in the end steered clear of the area of depersonalization.[14]) It was striking to Weiss that Freud only discussed his own experience of derealization on the Acropolis in reference to his father, not his mother, and Weiss took this to mean that Freud had "not understood his childhood."

As a matter of course I asked Weiss: *What did he think of Jones's books on Freud*? (I will be italicizing any direct questions of mine.) Weiss swept Jones aside as "unreliable," without conceding anything to my proposal that the problem could have been Jones's not being Jewish; Weiss instead highlighted the way he personally had those fifty letters from Freud. Weiss knew how large a role Jones had himself played in the politics of the psychoanalytic movement, and that Freud had written often to Jones too. (Only in 1993, with the final publication of the complete correspondence between Freud and Jones, did we find out that they had exchanged some 671 letters.[15]) But Weiss's objections to Jones were specific: although he had given Jones photostats of Weiss's Freud letters, he had only asked that Jones get specific permission before using them.[16] Jones, however, "did not bother, and just published whatever he wanted," afterwards turning over the letters to Freud's son Ernst. Weiss felt that he thereby had lost control over the content of these letters; he was concerned that there was a lot of material there on patients, including names, that he would not want published. (Subsequently there would be a major debate in the literature over the propriety of publishing patients' names.[17] In partial defense of how Jones dealt with Weiss, it should be noted that he was dying as he was completing that third volume of his Freud biography, and that could help mitigate his high-handed way of proceeding with Weiss's material.)

Of all the various clinical issues Weiss discussed with Freud, those pertaining to the problems of "Frank" played a central-seeming role; part of Weiss's special interest in "Frank" was that this young patient suffered from potency problems. Freud, who saw "Frank" once for a consultation with Weiss, had thought that as a result of psychoanalytic treatment "Frank" would become potent, but that he would not enjoy sex very much; Weiss had to be struck with how in fact Freud had failed to make a good prognosis about "Frank," since he did come to take keen pleasure in sexuality. Weiss was impressed with how "Freud himself, according to Jones, had no difficulty in his relationships with women friends"; such self-restraint in Freud seemed to Weiss striking, and a sign of Freud's own lack of interest in sex. According to Freud's view of "Frank," he had "sublimated so well" that it accounted for Freud's prediction about "Frank's" future unconcern with sex; but since Freud had not adequately understood "Frank," it might have been because he had been thinking about himself and the course of his own successful sublimations taking the place of sex. Although critics of Freud, including Jung and Wilhelm Reich, took issue with Freud's approach to creativity,[18] which was inclined to see sublimation at least partly as an alternative expression for sexuality, in this area Weiss was being loyally faithful to what he saw as Freud's intellectual intentions.

Weiss had other specific memories of Freud's exact comments, aside from that memorable 1930 meeting at his apartment, that stood out in Weiss's mind. The last time Weiss saw Freud was in Vienna during the summer of 1937. Hitler's successes in Germany made Freud pessimistic about the political future; he said he "did not like the way the world was going," and added that he was an old man (eighty-one) and glad of it. Freud meant he had not long to live and would be spared witnessing some of the coming disasters. Weiss reassured Freud that younger people did not like the times either, to which Freud had replied: "It is right for the young to protest, they should, but not correct for the old to complain."

Weiss's own direct links to Freud long preceded Anna Freud's own eventual rise to power within Freud's world, and by 1965 he and she were no longer on good terms. For him to say to me that "she was ambivalent about her father" was to pre-empt any possible criticism that he had himself strayed too far from the fold. (Subsequently, after some of the extent of Weiss's help to my work became evident, he would be publicly accused of "ambivalence to Freud,"[19] as if that were a special offense if not crime.) Weiss was pleased to rely on the word of an old Viennese analyst in New York, Herman Nunberg, who privately insisted that Freud would not have liked it at all that Anna had given Freud's love letters to his future wife for Jones's biographical use. (Nunberg's reputation for impeccable orthodoxy made him seem to Weiss an unimpeachable source, and therefore one which, unlike himself, could not be questioned even by the most devout. Nunberg, also analyzed by Federn, was notoriously snippish and waspish, and even though he grew more embittered with age he nonetheless continued to attract prominent pupils. He proved to be one of the most stubbornly difficult people I ever interviewed, and when for example I mentioned Weiss's name to Nunberg he at first skeptically asked "which Weiss?," since before World War I an almost unknown Karl Weiss, not a relation of Edoardo's, also presented material at the Vienna Psychoanalytic Society.)

Weiss maintained that Anna had "never overcome her father complex," and that she had been "married spiritually to her father." Both of these characterizations implied, in the lingo of traditional psychoanalytic terminology, that she failed to outgrow infantile attitudes, and was therefore stuck in neurosis. Weiss did know of Anna's courtship by Jones, but not about any other disciples of Freud in her romantic life. According to Weiss, Anna had been "trying to continue" to maintain the existence of "her father through her work." In his 1964 book, Weiss had written about how "by sharing their fathers' interests and hobbies, some women feel spiritually united with their fathers."[20]

Anna had also been, although Weiss seemed genuinely unsure about the wisdom of telling me this, analyzed by Freud himself. Weiss was to be one of the first to report this news to me, but when I came to publish it in 1969 I deliberately left his name out of my list of sources.[21] I felt that given his role as an outsider in Chicago, and the problems he thought he had with Anna already, he was not in a strong enough position to be able to take any subsequent criticisms about having made this disclosure. In fact, however, no matter how discreet I thought I had been in following his wishes for anonymity on this issue, by the time my material appeared in print he mailed me a copy of Freud's letter to him on the subject of his analysis of Anna.

Weiss had written to Freud to ask if Weiss should analyze his older son. In the late 1980s I found out that Weiss actually started analyzing the son, who told me he had easily and quickly—without hard feelings—rejected the intrusion into his privacy by his father. Freud had replied to Weiss's inquiry by saying that he hesitated to think that the analysis would work; it was in that context that Freud told Weiss that he had analyzed his own daughter, and that it "went" successfully, but with a son it might be different. Weiss was so worried about his being disloyal to the orthodox powers then prevalent professionally that although he often talked to me about this 1935 letter of Freud's, he never actually showed it to me during my interviewing. It then seemed to me an amusing sign of the impossibility of ever fully satisfying living witnesses that after my own studied disclosure of the analysis, Weiss asked why I had not mentioned the letter. By then Weiss's volume of letters from Freud was already in press.

Despite Weiss's eagerness not to provoke needlessly the establishment in analysis, he was nevertheless for his time emancipated as an analyst, as indicated even earlier by his reserved reception at the Menninger Clinic in Topeka. Weiss must have been the first among the Freudians to speak well to me of the work of Jung, although Weiss failed to mention his wife's clinical practice in Berkeley. In 1935 Freud had tried to warn Weiss that "less importance should be given to the term 'complex.'"[22] Jung had introduced "complex" into the psychoanalytic literature before World War I, and then Freud, after the falling out with Jung, felt forever frustrated about being stuck with it. To me Weiss dismissed the accusation that Jung was an anti-Semite, and argued, as Jung had too, that the reason Jung accepted a psychiatric editorial post in Germany after Hitler's coming to power in 1933 was to ensure that the analytic literature could still appear under the Nazis.[23] Freud had chosen Jung as his heir apparent in the first place precisely because he was a Gentile, able to rescue psychoanalysis from being exclusively a Jewish movement, and Freud later tended to continue to favor Gentiles as future analytic leaders. But after the break between Freud and Jung, Freud had in print accused Jung of having had anti-Semitic prejudices against him.[24]

Weiss acknowledged that there was "lots of mysticism in Jung," but Weiss maintained that it was not all "astrology and palm-reading." Jung importantly proposed, for example, that a dream could be interpreted on a subject as well as an object level; that is, anyone in a dream may stand for an aspect of the dreamer himself, and not just a former love object. By 1965, American analysts were concerned with "ego symbols" in dreams, without knowing that Jung had anticipated this approach; and followers of Kohut's concern with the self would be similarly extending an approach Jung (and also Federn) first initiated. Weiss went on to cite another interesting idea of Jung's: his concept of the "anima" meant than a man who dreams of a woman who is very sad may be expressing thereby some of his own sadness. Jung's notion of an "anima" in men, and an "animus" in women, was a way of Jung's intriguingly talking about psychological bisexuality, a theme that Freud was also absorbed with. In addition, Weiss thought that Jung's term "persona," how we present ourselves to the outside world, was another good idea, in that it highlighted the dangers of conformism, something Erich Fromm and R. D. Laing would also be concerned with. According to Jung the task of psychotherapy was to release the patient's truest self, and Donald Winnicott was one of the rare Freudians to acknowledge how Jung had preceded him on this point. For Weiss Jung's concept of a "shadow," the bad side behind the "persona," also seemed valuable; Jung was not, as Freud had polemically charged, repudiating the concept of the unconscious but instead taking a different approach to it. The key issue was always what one puts into the content of the unconscious.[25]

It took an unusual amount of quiet courage for Weiss in 1965 to be as generous as he was about what Jung's successfully added to the history of the field. Even today Jung's contributions remain almost as hotly contested as those of Freud. Weiss alluded with me to the existence within psychoanalysis of an "Index" of prohibited books, which included those of Jung. We have already cited evidence for the trouble that arose for Weiss in Topeka because of his open-mindedness about Jung's creation of what he called "analytic psychology." (Freud himself always referred to Jung's work as representative of the "Zurich school.") But for Weiss as early as 1942 to have put in print the statement that "I am too unfamiliar with the Jungian psychology to be able to take up a precise attitude toward it,"[26] was to guarantee difficulty with those like Freud's daughter Anna who inherited Freud's mantle.

Weiss thought it evidence on the issue of the old charge about Jung's alleged anti-Semitism that Erich Neumann, a "favorite pupil" of Jung's, was a Jew who lived for years in Tel Aviv. But Jung's anti-Semitism would not necessarily have been inconsistent with his being on good terms with some individual Jews; it took awhile until some of my own research convinced me of the degree of truth in the charge about Jung's anti-Semitism.[27] I do not think that Weiss would have been able, since he lost so many close relatives in the Holocaust, to acknowledge the genuineness of Jung's collaboration with the Nazis and at the same time maintain that Jung's ideas were being unduly neglected. Jungians have themselves been facing up recently to Jung's dreadful politics in the 1930s, without its meaning that they abandon his genuine contributions to modern psychology; but this has been taking place several decades after my interviews with Weiss.

Besides inquiring about the subject of Freud's relationship with Jung, I wanted to know: *What sorts of other mistakes were in Jones*? Weiss got impatient and was not much interested in trying to explore this subject with me, except to say that there were "lots" of such errors. Weiss thought I should, as long as I was visiting in Chicago, consult with Bruno Bettelheim about Jones, and I did as Weiss recommended.[28] Bettelheim had in fact been brave enough to have published a couple of the first critiques of Jones, and as someone younger Weiss thought Bettelheim would be interested in straightening out further historiographical problems associated with Freud's life.

Notes

1. "Introduction to Edoardo Weiss's *Elements of Psychoanalysis*," *Standard Edition*, (London: The Hogarth Press, 1953-74), vol. 21, p. 256.
2. April 27, 1932. I am indebted to the help of Michael Shroeter for this unpublished quotation from the extensive Freud-Eitingon correspondence Shroeter is editing.
3. "On the History of the Psychoanalytic Movement," *Standard Edition*, vol. 14, p. 33.
4. *The Diary of Sigmund Freud 1929-1939: A Record of the Final Decade* (New York: Charles Scribner's Sons, 1992), p. 286.
5. Ibid., p. 88; *The Letters of Sigmund Freud and Arnold Zweig*, ed. Ernst L. Freud, translated by Prof. and Mrs. W. D. Robson-Scott (London: The Hogarth Press, 1970), p. 108.
6. *The Complete Correspondence of Sigmund Freud and Ernest Jones 1908-1939*, ed. R. Andrew Paskauskas (Cambridge, MA: Harvard University Press, 1993), p. 739.
7. Edoardo Weiss, *Agoraphobia in the Light of Ego Psychology* (New York: Grune and Stratton, 1964).
8. Theodor Reik, *Listening With the Third Ear* (New York: Farrar, Straus, and Co., 1948), pp. 15-16.

9. *The Complete Correspondence of Sigmund Freud and Karl Abraham 1907-1925*, edited Ernst Falzeder, translated by Caroline Schwarzacher (London: Karmac, 2002), p. 92.
10. Weiss, *Agoraphobia in the Light of Ego Psychology*, pp. 69-81.
11. Paul Roazen, *Freud and His Followers* (New York: Alfred A. Knopf, 1975), pp. 246-50.
12. I am indebted to a private communication from Dr. Anna Maria Accerboni.
13. *Standard Edition*, Vol. 22, pp. 239-48.
14. Anna Freud, *The Ego and the Mechanisms of Defence*, authorized translation by Cecil Baines (London: The Hogarth Press, 1954).
15. *The Complete Correspondence of Sigmund Freud and Ernest Jones 1908-1939.*
16. Edoardo Weiss to Ernest Jones, May 22, 1956 (Library of Congress).
17. Gerhard Fichtner, "Kritische Glosse," *Psyche*, August 1994, pp. 738-45; Andre Haynal, "Diskussion," *Psyche*, Feb. 1995, pp. 174-181, also K. R. Eissler, *Psyche*, Feb. 1995, pp. 182-83. See also Paul Roazen, "Ethics and Privacy," in *The Trauma of Freud*, op. cit., pp. 111-127, and Ernst Falzeder, "Preface," *The Complete Correspondence of Sigmund Freud and Karl Abraham 1907-1925*, pp. ix-xvii .
18. Anthony Storr, *The Dynamics of Creation* (New York: Atheneum, 1972).
19. Kurt R. Eissler, *Victor Tausk's Suicide* (New York: International Universities Press, 1983), p. 76.
20. Weiss, *Agoraphobia in the Light of Ego Psychology*, p. 26.
21. Paul Roazen, "Freud's Analysis of Anna," in *The Death of Psychoanalysis: Murder, Suicide, or Rumor Greatly Exaggerated*, ed. Robert Prince (Northvale, NJ: Jason Aronson, 1999), pp. 141-51. Also see Roazen, *On the Freud Watch: Public Memoirs* (London: Free Association Books, 2003), ch. 3, pp. 41-50.
22. Edoardo Weiss, *Sigmund Freud as a Consultant: Recollections of a Pioneer in Psychoanalysis*, with an introduction by Martin Grotjahn (New York: Intercontinental Medical Book Corporation, 1970; New Brunswick, NJ: Transaction Publishers, 1991), p. 75. See also *The Freud Journal of Lou Andreas-Salomé*, translated by Stanley A. Leavy (New York: Basic Books, 1964), pp. 38-39. See too "On the History of the Psychoanalytic Movement," *Standard Edition*, vol. 14, p. 29.
23. Paul Roazen, "Erich Fromm's Exclusion from the IPA," in *Cultural Foundations of Political Psychology* (New Brunswick, NJ: Transaction Publishers, 2003), Ch. 1, pp. 1-34.
24. "On the History of the Psychoanalytic Movement," p. 43.
25. Paul Roazen, "Interviews on Freud and Jung with Henry A. Murray in 1965," *Journal of Analytical Psychology*, January 2003, pp. 1-27.
26. Edoardo Weiss, "Psychic Defence and the Technique of Its Analysis," *International Journal of Psychoanalysis*, vol. 23, part 1 (1942), p. 77.
27. Paul Roazen, *The Trauma of Freud: Controversies in Psychoanalysis* (New Brunswick, NJ: Transaction Publishers, 2002), pp. 35-43.

28. See Paul Roazen, "The Rise and Fall of Bruno Bettelheim," in *Political Theory and the Psychology of the Unconscious* (London: Open Gate Press, 2000), pp. 124-51.

4

Pioneering Under Mussolini

If I failed with Weiss in getting him to open up more by mentioning Jones's biographical work, I succeeded better by being interested in the history of psychoanalysis in Italy. An Italian by the name of Dr. Marco Levi-Bianchini, like Weiss also Jewish but from Venice, was in Weiss's view a "fake" whom Freud had maddeningly refused to spot. It had to be permanently galling to Weiss that in his pamphlet *On the History of the Psychoanalytic Movement* Freud had, in 1923, added a footnote how in Italy both Levi-Bianchini and Weiss had "come forward as translators and champions of psychoanalysis."[1]

Levi-Bianchini had first written to Freud from near Naples even before the time when Weiss had started to practice in Trieste after World War I. Freud granted Levi-Bianchini's request to have permission to publish in Italy Freud's *Introductory Lectures on Psychoanalysis*, one of Freud's great texts, in what was to be a psychoanalytic series; shortly after World War I Weiss had himself already made the draft of a translation into Italian, but Freud had said to him that he better get in touch with Levi-Bianchini and withdraw in his favor. Weiss did as he was told and wrote an Introduction for Levi-Bianchini's edition, but when the book came out there were, Weiss said, hundreds of mistakes in the original proofs that were subsequently allowed to get into print. Afterwards, when Weiss explained to Freud the extent of these errors, Freud wrote Weiss a mollifying letter about Levi-Bianchini, saying that there were both good as well as bad qualities in him. Weiss remained historically tethered to Levi-Bianchini, and both got later made "honorary" members of the post-World War II Italian Psychoanalytic Society, although Levi-Bianchini had died by the mid-1960s. On his own Weiss published in Italy translations of writings by Freud like *Totem and Taboo*, *The New Introductory Lectures on Psychoanalysis*, as well as "The Moses of Michelangelo."

Weiss insisted that Levi-Bianchini had been a thorn in his side in Italy, "a real fraud." He had signed himself "professor" when he initially wrote to Freud, and Freud was so absolutely delighted that he had invited him to a meal at his home in Vienna, although Freud's wife Martha had not been present. Even this limited hospitality ran counter to how rarely Freud ever entertained guests. But in actuality Levi-Bianchini only had a lowly academic position, perhaps equivalent to what Americans call an "assistant professor." He nonetheless even claimed to have "founded" a psychoanalytic society in Italy, but he did so by listing the names of his assistants at a sanatorium who according to Weiss "had never even heard of Freud."

Although it was not until later, long after all my meetings with Weiss, that I made the discovery, Levi-Bianchini had in fact become a member of the Vienna Psychoanalytic Society in 1921. He also spoke about the position of psychoanalysis in Italy at the 1922 Berlin IPA Congress, where Weiss also gave a clinical paper. Levi-Bianchini was a successful self-promoter, in contrast to how reserved Weiss could be; so in 1930 Levi-Bainchini attended the First International Congress in Mental Hygiene in Washington, D.C., a notable event in the reception of psychoanalysis in America.

From Weiss's point of view, the spread of psychoanalysis in Italy was hampered by Freud's credulity about Levi-Bianchini, as well as the problems created by some other unreliable types Freud allowed himself to be taken in by. For example, Freud saw some newspaper people who afterwards wrote pieces that were disappointing. In general the Italian psychiatrists remained hostile to all things that appeared to be German, and the old Austrian influence was still widely resented; anti-Semitism also remained an obstacle. Italian neurologists would only praise Freud for his prepsychoanalytic neurological writings. And of course the Church's opposition to Freud endured as a difficulty too; it eventually succeeded in closing down the psychoanalytic journal Weiss had inaugurated in 1932.

Weiss was especially resentful of one point in Jones's biography of Freud that bore on the history of analysis in Italy, and this incident has acquired a permanent-seeming place in the history books. Weiss had, after moving from Trieste to Rome in 1931, in analysis with him a daughter of a high official, Giovacchino Forzano, who was a playwright and movie producer as well as a Cabinet member in Mussolini's government. (Recently a book about Forzano's theatrical works has appeared in English.[2]) Weiss took the patient, Concetta Forzano, whom in print he called "Ethel,"[3] when he was having some difficulties with her, for a consultation with Freud in Vienna; and her father, who according to some had become a mere mouthpiece for Mussolini but had a play on in Vienna, came along as well.

At the 1933 interview Forzano gave Freud a dedicated copy of one of his plays co-authored with Mussolini, and asked Freud for a signed photograph, as well as for an inscribed book to be given to Mussolini, Forzano's old friend. Freud, not without some subtle irony, picked a recent little volume of his public exchange of letters with Albert Einstein titled *Why War*? At the time Weiss was very embarrassed because he thought that Freud was obliged for Weiss's sake and in behalf of the Italian Psychoanalytic Society to consent to his patient's father's request. For Freud to have refused such a dedication would have hurt Weiss's position in Italy. Freud had chosen to write something gracious about what Mussolini had done for excavating and reconstructing archeological sites in Italy from the Roman past: "Benito Mussolini with the respectful greetings of an old man who recognizes in the ruler the cultural hero."[4] (Jones's version of what Freud had put in the flyleaf of the book was: "From an old man who greets in the Ruler the Hero of Culture."[5])

Still another alternative translation of what Freud inscribed reads: "To Benito Mussolini, with the humble greetings of an old man who recognizes in the man of power the champion of culture."[6] As one Italian analyst, wholly sympathetic to Freud, has put it: "The phrasing of Freud's inscription to Mussolini is unequivocal, and Weiss's attempt to play down its significance and importance is quite ineffectual."[7] Two months later Mussolini was hardly won over; he then wrote his only public reference to Freud: "Life is more and more difficult, and Communism more and more complicated. To follow it one needs to be competent in that new science or imposture called psychoanalysis, whose Pontifex Maximus is the Viennese professor Freud."[8]

Weiss, for all the independence of his later position in the States, was naturally worried when I knew him about what others had made of Freud's willingness to write such a dedication to Mussolini. Alfred Adler, who was a dedicated socialist and became one of the early renegades in Freud's movement, did have a follower who picked up on Freud's collaborative-sounding deed.[9] Adler was himself so bitter about his falling out with Freud that he thought psychoanalysis's thriving helped explain the success of Fascism; Freud fully reciprocated Adler's ill-feelings.

Jones himself embellished (Weiss said "lied") about the significant facts associated with this particular patient of Weiss's, because Jones claimed that after the Nazis entered Austria in 1938 Weiss was in a position to be "in near contact with the Duce."[10] One of Weiss's students in Rome did have, we now know, one of the "Duce's" relatives in analysis. Subsequently another orthodox analyst, following Jones's lead, wrote that Weiss "knew Mussolini."[11] Even an independent-minded analyst reiterated that "Mussolini was active due to the influence of Edoardo Weiss in Rome."[12] Weiss did once succeed in having a 1934 audience with Mussolini's son-in-law Galeazzo Ciano, who at the time was undersecretary of the Ministry of Press and Propaganda and a future foreign minister, in connection with the Fascist ban on the publication of Weiss's psychoanalytic journal. Press censorship and the suppression of academic freedom were part of Mussolini's regime, which also intervened against the republican side in the Spanish Civil War set off by General Franco's insurrection.

In print Weiss seems to have referred to having through Forzano "obtained an introduction to a government secretary in order to discuss with him the threatened suspension of our journal."[13] But perhaps Weiss could have used Ciano's name in writing to Freud, who also mentioned to Weiss the assistance of "the secretary" Weiss had seen.[14] A distinguished historian has recently written that "for years Ciano remained the dictator's favorite, until in 1944 his father-in-law had him shot in the back on a trumped-up charge of treachery."[15]

But according to Jones's published version, Weiss told Jones in connection with the 1938 rescue of Freud and his entourage from Nazi-occupied Austria "that Mussolini...made a *demarché*, either directly to Hitler or to his Ambassador in Vienna. [A *demarché* would mean a formal diplomatic message.] Probably he remembered the compliment Freud had paid him four years before."[16] It should probably not be surprising that written history can get built on the kind of power-obsessed fantasy about Weiss and Mussolini that Jones successfully set going; so that an independent historian has also been capable of writing that after the Nazi *Anschluss* in Austria "even Mussolini is supposed to have put in an official word" for Freud.[17]

But Weiss insisted to me that Jones had wholly invented the "near contact" between himself and Mussolini, and that Weiss had had a strict record of anti-Fascism. (A past president of the Italian Psychoanalytic, writing of Weiss's connection with the Forzanos, said of Weiss that he was "perhaps a bit pedantic academically but spotlessly honest...."[18]) During World War I Weiss's sympathies had been with Italy, because he felt that Italy was more democratic than the Hapsburgs. After the war, when Mussolini came to power in 1922, Weiss was terribly upset. He was clearly against this dictatorship, or any such regime, and he was uncompromising. Trieste had to suffer under fascist rule, since the regime was anti-Slav and hostile to minorities; Weiss's wife and her whole family were Croatian. Weiss left Trieste for Rome after having refused to buckle under to Fascist demands on how he might continue with his professional Triestine hospital position. Weiss was able to be very helpful to his elder son Emilio, for once Mussolini's racial policies were put in place, the young man was confronted with the many problems of emigration. Emilio reported that he did not have to contend with the trauma of rejection, which was common among young people from families who were not clearly opposed to Mussolini.[19]

It is true that Giovacchino Forzano had gotten the ban on Weiss's journal temporarily lifted, but then a powerful Franciscan psychiatrist at the new Catholic University in Milan, Agostino Gemelli (1878-1959), had again forced the withdrawal of Weiss's publication.[20] Other Vatican opponents also worked against Weiss. (Weiss remained not as sure as Jones that Father Gemelli was responsible for the suppression.) But Weiss insisted that he was never in any direct way in touch with Mussolini, only once saw him at a distance, and not Jones's source for such an idea as "near contact." Concetta Forzano did say to Weiss that Mussolini had in 1938 sent a message to Vienna in Freud's behalf, but Weiss himself had no evidence as to the truth of such an intervention; her father also told

Weiss that Mussolini had written Hitler about Freud, but Weiss thought it could not have been so and for all he knew Mussolini had done nothing whatever.

I think that Jones, who was in general overly impressed by powerful leaders, was probably also taken in by some fantasies of Freud's own that Mussolini was particularly concerned to protect him in Vienna. (I was told by a famous American psychologist, Henry A. Murray, that Jones, a fiery little man, had set up his study in the country in such a way that he had plenty of space to size someone up before they reached his desk—"just like Mussolini.") Behind Jones's back in London analysts there used to refer to him as Napoleon. But it always pleased Freud to think that a supporter of his had high political influence, and at that time Freud did not take an especially dim view of Mussolini.

As the socio-political upheavals in the late 1930s grew worse, and psychoanalysis got threatened both in Italy and in Vienna itself, Freud wrote that he was relying on the influence that he alleged that Weiss, as well as others, had. In 1934 Freud had written Arnold Zweig that Weiss had "direct access to Mussolini."[21] Mussolini then appeared to be a protector of Austrian independence from Hitler's Germany. Freud's attitude toward Mussolini was like that of many others throughout the 1920s and 1930s when Mussolini attracted a lot of support and admiration, even among American progressives, from outside Italy. In *Civilization and Its Discontents* (1930), before Freud inscribed *Why War?* for Mussolini, Freud had complained that America had failed to produce super-ego "leader-type" men.[22]

Although most foreign observers who had been inclined to be sympathetic to Mussolini were repelled by the Italian dictator's 1935 invasion of Abyssinia, Freud could still write in his *Moses and Monotheism* (1938) that "with similar violence" to what the Soviets were then using in Russia "the Italian people are being trained up to orderliness and a sense of duty."[23] According to Weiss, Freud did not think much of the Italian national character; it would have been typical for the Viennese of Freud's generation, who grew up in the days of the Hapsburg Empire, to look down on Italians.

By 1938 Freud had some special reasons for wanting to think well of Mussolini. Only in the summer of 1938, after Freud had left Vienna for London, England, had Mussolini adopted within Italy

Hitler's policies against the Jews, which were finally to drive Weiss to the States. The Italian anti-Semitic campaign officially began in July, and the next month "the sudden announcement of Italy's anti-Semitic laws made the state of Mussolini's mental health not a matter of 'hints' but of serious speculation" among American newspaper correspondents.[24] Right up until the German takeover of Austria it had been common for Viennese Jews to have been relying on Italy to protect Austrian autonomy.

Freud had special reasons of his own not to want to face up to the realities of Mussolini. Freud, I believe, feared that once he left he would be without his doctors in Vienna; they had been handling his jaw cancer since 1923, and it could be anticipated that without them his medical condition would likely deteriorate. In London the physicians, who did not know his case, were intimidated by his fame there and hesitated to operate in time. He went downhill pretty fast in England. I think that it was partly for the sake of staying in Vienna that Freud had, over the opposition of some of his favorite pupils, expressed support for an authoritarian regime in Austria, even after it had repressed a socialist uprising in a bloody civil war. Freud was of course extremely old; but it remains noteworthy that it was in London that he finally put in press *Moses and Monotheism*, containing the relatively favorable mention of Mussolini. Like other of Freud's pupils Weiss ignored the reference to Mussolini, and merely assessed the book itself as "not very accurate." Weiss conceded that *Moses and Monotheism* was more important for understanding Freud's personal psychology than for comprehending Moses.

Towards the end of his stay in Vienna Freud maintained several significant lifelines abroad. Freud's analysand the Princess George, Marie Bonaparte, could be relied on by him in Paris since she had royal connections and abundant money. Jones in London knew expertly which strings there to pull politically in Freud's behalf. The American Ambassador to France then, William C. Bullitt, was a former patient of Freud's; independently of Bullitt, when the Nazis marched into Vienna we know that the American undersecretary of state, Sumner Welles, cabled to the American consul in Vienna about Freud's safety in behalf of Roosevelt's Administration. And Ruth Mack Brunswick, still another disciple of Freud's, was well connected in New Deal circles through her jurist father.[25]

Throughout Freud's last years in Vienna he had, in defiance of Austrian currency regulations, kept money deposited abroad. An intelligent Viennese had an incentive to do likewise, and many evidently did exactly that. When the Gestapo took Anna Freud for a day in Vienna it was almost certainly to inquire about the state of Freud's finances, since her brother Martin had somehow left incriminating documents in the office of the psychoanalytic press. Despite how much, as Freud wrote, the Nazis had "bled" him, his finances had been handled shrewdly enough so that he did not die poor in London.[26]

Mythmaking about Freud has been abetted by the credulity of his followers, which in turn has been promoted by the unnecessary secrecy about documents. We do at least know, thanks to the research of one Italian analyst, that Forzano, "Ethel's" father, did in fact write to Mussolini on Freud's behalf. Amidst the Duce's private correspondence there is a letter from Forzano dated March 14, 1938: "I recommend to Your Excellency a glorious old man of eighty-two who greatly admires Your Excellency: Freud, a Jew." (The Nazi occupation of Austria took place on March 11th.) Forzano's intercession with Mussolini has therefore succeeded in being preserved. It seems to me noteworthy that at least one Italian analyst believed that "considering Mussolini's habits and the situation of the time, it is likely that Mussolini did in fact intervene."[27]

Weiss, however, took no direct part in contacting Mussolini, although "Ethel" remained in analysis with him until close to his departure for the States in early 1939. Jones was so eager to place Freud among the mighty, perhaps following Freud's so far largely unpublished versions of his protectors abroad, that it was not evident to Jones that it did not add to Freud's reputation to have him relying on Mussolini at such a late date. But the tendency to romanticize about Freud's politics is still so common that even those influenced by Herbert Marcuse, and other readings of Freud that have flowed from the Marxist Frankfurt school of critical sociology, do not even acknowledge the existence of this particular ethical dilemma.

Nothing in the Freud-Mussolini story can equal the unfortunate details of Jung's own collaboration with the Nazis; yet Freud, Jones, and Anna Freud themselves behaved less than heroically in trying to "salvage" psychoanalysis within post-1933 Hitlerian Germany.[28] Yet by World War II a debate would rage about what were the sources within Western culture for the rise of Fascism. The philosopher Nietzsche would take some of the blame for what had happened in that his program for going "beyond good and evil," and his assault on Christian ethics in particular, may have helped undermine Western standards of morality. Freud too shared many of Nietzsche's views.[29] It is in this connection that Adler's private reproach against Freud for helping the rise of the Nazis seems to me noteworthy.

It is possible, and necessary, to weigh the implications of the politics of psychoanalysts. I have, for example, long thought it was telling about Freud's conservative inclinations that in *The Interpretation of Dreams* he so readily identified with the victims of the French Revolution's Reign of Terror. His eagerness to think well of Mussolini, and the interest Jones had in helping to publicize the story, should tell us something about the nature of the ethical commitments of that first generation of analysts. For example, Wilhelm Reich, who had boldly denounced Jung at the outset of his collaboration with the Nazis, was informed by Jones in London that Reich had to choose between politics and psychoanalysis. An IPA analyst like Eitingon in Berlin was mainly worried that Reich might get arrested on property of the psychoanalytic institute there, endangering the German psychoanalytic movement as a whole. Jones, like others at the time, had found it appropriate to work with Herman Göring's distant cousin, the psychiatrist Dr. Matthias Göring, even after Freud's teachings were officially banned in Nazi Germany. Alleged analytic neutrality often masks a commitment to an authoritarian status quo, which is also true of today's most up-to-date-sounding involvement in the latest in biological psychiatry's psychopharmacology. Ethics are necessarily intimately intertwined with all branches of psychology, which should ensure the continued vitality of the whole vexed subject of psychology and politics.

As a historian I am grateful for learning the added details Italian analysts have provided us with; now we know that Forzano did in fact do something in Freud's behalf, although that still does not amount to Weiss having known Mussolini, nor been "in near contact" with him; and Weiss stoutly maintained to me that he had never told Jones anything about Mussolini having intervened for Freud. When Weiss and I came across the name Forzano in his papers, he admonished me to "forget" I had ever seen it and I never put it into print; although on occasion I did look at the Indexes to new books about Mussolini to see if there was anything there about Forzano, my inquisitiveness was inhibited by Weiss's injunction to me and I am convinced that Weiss would be shocked at the revelations made public by analysts recently.

Myth-making about Freud can go on unchecked as along as idealizations about him are uncorrected. Few of us now would approve of his having flattered Mussolini in any way, even though in the context of those times and the state of Freud's health it may be more understandable how Freud could have reacted that way. The whole tradition of thought Freud started has been politically on the naïve side, although Jung may have been politically dumber than most. Both Freud and Jung were capable of acting opportunistically in behalf of their respective work.

In a situation like we find ourselves in, without adequate access to the appropriate documents, mythologizing can all too often flourish. It is precisely this sort of context that promotes indiscretion, since inevitably we are so hungry for finding out what actually happened. So as intellectual historians we can sometimes be grateful for violations of psychoanalytic propriety. The superiority of one piece of historical research over another is often established by who has been the most successful as a truth-teller.

But psychoanalysts must remember that they get paid for being discreet, and betraying the confidentiality of patients' names is for them bound to be a questionable procedure. When I first published *Brother Animal: The Story of Freud and Tausk* in 1969, and mentioned Herbert Lehman's name as a patient Federn had traveled to America for treatment before World War I, I was doing so as a young intellectual historian, not an analyst; it was long after Lehman had died, it did no harm, and betrayed no professional standards on my part.[30] My *Helene Deutsch: A Psychoanalyst's Life*[31] was written many years later, and with her authorization; I found then that I implicitly identified with what she would have wanted me to remain silent about, and out of loyalty to her, for example, I failed to interview some former private analytic patients of hers (not in training analyses), even some that she put into published case histories, because I felt she would not have wanted me to transgress the norms that are opposed to the violation of a patient's privacy. I hope I retained my objectivity towards Helene Deutsch; but I feel just as deferential towards the memory of Edoardo Weiss as to Helene

Deutsch, and what they each would have approved of, which is why I am now raising the troublesome question of psychoanalysis and ethics in connection with the historical linkages between Weiss, Freud, and Mussolini.

Notes

1. Sigmund Freud, "On the History of the Psychoanalytic Movement," *Standard Edition*, vol. 14 (London: The Hogarth Press, 1953-74), p. 34.
2. C. E. J. Griffiths, *The Theatrical Works of Giovacchino Forzano: Drama for Mussolini's Italy* (Ceredigion, Wales: Mellen, 2000).
3. Edoardo Weiss, *Agoraphobia in the Light of Ego Psychology* (New York: Grune and Stratton, 1964), pp. 54-63.
4. Edoardo Weiss, *Sigmund Freud as a Consultant*: *Recollections of a Pioneer in Psychoanalysis*, with an introduction by Martin Grotjahn (New York: Intercontinental Medical Book Corporation, 1970; New Brunswick, NJ: Transaction Publishers, 1991), p. 20.
5. Ernest Jones, *Life and Work of Sigmund Freud*, Vol. 3: *The Last Phase* (New York: Basic Books, 1957), p. 180.
6. Glauco Carloni, "Freud and Mussolini: A Minor Drama in Two Acts, One Interlude, and Five Characters," *L'Italia nella Psicoanalisis, Italy in Psychoanalysis* (1989), p. 52.
7. Ibid., p. 53.
8. Ibid., p. 54.
9. Alfred Adler, *Superiority and Social Interest*, ed. Heinz L. Ansbacher and Rowena R. Ansbacher, third revised edition (New York: W.W. Norton, 1979), p. 320.
10. Jones, *Life and Work of Sigmund Freud*, Vol. 3, pp. 220-21.
11. Max Schur, *Freud: Living and Dying* (New York: International Universities Press, 1972), p. 498.
12. Richard Sterba, *Reminiscences of a Viennese Psychoanalyst* (Detroit, MI: Wayne State University Press, 1982), p. 164.
13. Weiss, *Sigmund Freud as a Consultant*, p. 79.
14. Ibid., p. 80.
15. Denis Mack Smith, *Modern Italy: A Political History* (Ann Arbor: University of Michigan Press, 1997), pp. 341.
16. Jones, *Life and Work of Sigmund Freud*, Vol. III, p. 221.
17. Hannah S. Decker, *Freud, Dora, and Vienna 1900* (New York: The Free Press, 1991), p. 184.
18. Carloni, "Freud and Mussolini," p. 51.
19. Letter of Emilio Weiss to Paul Roazen, Jan. 22, 1982.
20. I am indebted to Daria Colombo for sharing her "Psychoanalysis and the Catholic Church: The Role of Father Gemelli in Shaping Italy's Response to Freud's Work: 1925-1953," Journal of the History of the Behavioral Sciences, Vol. 39, No 4 (Fall 2003), pp. 333-480.

21. *The Letters of Sigmund Freud and Arnold Zweig*, ed. Ernst L. Freud (London: The Hogarth Press, 1970), p. 92.
22. John P. Diggins, *Mussolini and Fascism: The View From America* (Princeton, NJ: Princeton University Press, 1972), p. 72.
23. "Moses and Monotheism," *Standard Edition*, vol. 23, p. 54.
24. Diggins, op. cit., pp. 318-19. See also Meir Michaelis, *Mussolini and the Jews: German-Italian Relations and the Jewish Question in Italy* (Oxford: The Clarendon Press, 1978).
25. Paul Roazen, *Freud and His Followers* (New York: Alfred A. Knopf, 1975), pp. 420-36; Paul Roazen, *How Freud Worked: First-Hand Accounts of Patients* (Northvale, NJ: Jason Aronson, 1995), pp. 31-88.
26. Paul Roazen, "Freud's Will," in *The Historiography of Psychoanalysis* (New Brunswick, NJ: Transaction Publishers, 2001), pp. 447-52.
27. Carloni, "Freud and Mussolini," p. 58.
28. Paul Roazen, "Erich Fromm's Exclusion From the IPA," in *Cultural Foundations of Political Psychology* (New Brunswick, NJ: Transaction Publishers, 2003).
29. Paul Roazen, "Nietzsche and Freud: Two Voices from the Underground," in *Political Theory and the Psychology of the Unconscious* (London: Open Gate Press, 2003)., pp. 28-48.
30. Paul Roazen, *Brother Animal: The Story of Freud and Tausk* (New York: Alfred A. Knopf, 1969; second edition, New Brunswick, NJ: Transaction Publishers, 1990), p. 152.
31. Paul Roazen, *Helene Deutsch: A Psychoanalyst's Life* (New York: Doubleday/Anchor, 1985; second edition, New Brunswick, NJ: Transaction Publishers, 1992).

5

Discipleship and Federn

Weiss was capable of using the word "dictator" for Freud, though as soon as the word once escaped from his mouth, he hesitated at his own boldness and corrected himself to soften the word down to the issue of Freud's having been "intolerant." Freud "allowed" the members of the Vienna Psychoanalytic Society to be "critical" of his works, but Weiss quickly went on to add, in a lowered voice, that "of course Freud did not accept" any such negative points. (It is worth remembering that Weiss officially entered on his own membership in Freud's "cause" after the public exclusion of Adler and while the breach with Jung was already privately established, though not yet publicly recognized.) Everyone in the Vienna group "had a right to speak." But as a consequence of these authoritarian attitudes on Freud's part, Weiss—like some others in the circle—was unhappy about the way Freud had only cited those of his loyal pupils who had confirmed his earlier findings. Since Wilhelm Stekel, for example, had first "discovered the death instinct," and later had a falling out with Freud, that meant that Freud would himself never use the term "Thanatos" precisely because Stekel himself had done so beforehand.[1]

Each of my interviews with Weiss would be rich ones, since he was so wide-ranging in what he wanted to talk about. He characteristically stuck portions of articles and manuscripts before me in order to illustrate points that he wanted to make, and only as time went on did I get to know something of him as a human being. However sure of himself Weiss had at first seemed to be, he struck me as unusually nice, and I later concluded that he was exceptionally compassionate. His not allowing me to leave my habitual copy of the daily *New York Times* in his waiting room before an interview was, the reader will recall, for fear it might upset a patient; Weiss continued to treat some unusually disturbed cases, and like other analysts he seemed to believe that continuity in the treatment setting was an important aspect of the therapeutic milieu. (In Weiss's time Freud's own waiting room before World War I had had a copy of a book by the humorist Wilhelm Busch[2]; one of Weiss's brothers, almost certainly Ottocaro, bought the same book for Weiss's own first waiting room back in Trieste. By the 1920s, when Freud had mainly Americans for patients, weeklies from the States like the *New Republic* were left for patients to read. Although by then the Busch was gone, today in the Freud House Museum in Vienna a copy of Busch has been put back in his old waiting room.)

In talking about Freud, Weiss relied on examples from his own clinical practice to illustrate his general points. Two of Weiss's current patients, one a Lutheran minister and the other a Catholic priest, were having conflicts with their faith; and both of them thought that Freud was "religious." Weiss too (like Freud's disciple Oskar Pfister, a Swiss pastor) considered that Freud was religious without knowing it; Pfister, who once stopped off for coffee in Rome at Weiss's, had the better of Pfister's argument with Freud, in Weiss's view, over the future of religion.[3] Only now do we now know that as a young man Freud was preoccupied with problems of philosophy and even theology.[4]

Weiss liked to stress that Freud was concerned with motivation that went beyond what could be currently explained scientifically. Weiss knew that Freud maintained his atheism yet at the same time very much wanted to be a Jew. Weiss thought that Freud had "mystical" tendencies of which he did not want to speak; for example, Freud could believe in telepathy, although he did not want to publish his beliefs for fear it would hurt analysis. (Even though many of the early analysts, such as Helene Deutsch, Sandor Ferenczi, and Edward Hitschmann wrote on telepathic matters, the subject still remains a forbidden one—even as a historical question—within the profession.) After meetings of the Vienna Psychoanalytic Society Weiss went with Freud and others to a coffee house, and in that informal atmosphere Freud mentioned his convictions about "thought transference." Freud thought that analysis had enough to contend with without loading it down with still further problems, a point we will come back to in connection with Freud's letters to Weiss.[5]

Weiss was himself open-minded about the possibility of the existence of telepathy, and more respectful of the nature of religious feelings than one might have expected in one of Freud's followers. The Freudian iconography in Weiss's office, which included the memorabilia about both Freud and Federn I have already mentioned, may have been in itself unusual, but that generation of faithful followers of Freud's usually had some reminders of their professional emotional commitments. Someone like Nunberg had in an entranceway to his apartment office a fresh-cut vase of flowers beneath a view of a picture of Freud. These ostensibly secular relics had, I came to think, a quasi-religious sort of significance.

After my first seeing Weiss, I then met some others in the Chicago analytic group, primarily those who were either European in origin or had been trained abroad, and then returned to interview Weiss again. As I have indicated, it turned out he was interested in my helping with his biography, one that he thought he could "dictate" to me. He did not have in mind an interpretive work, but something short he could use to satisfy those in Italy who were urging him to do something that they could publish about him. Weiss was not terribly expansive about his personal history, but proud of several concepts that he thought he had introduced into psychoanalysis in the course of his having not having written "much." He was surprised that Helene Deutsch, for example, was writing relatively little by the mid-1960s, while his own output still continued at a fairly steady pace.

Mainly my interviews with Weiss were about the early days of analysis in Italy. Therefore I did not inquire much about the current-day situation then in Chicago, although I believe I always told Weiss who else I had been seeing. Weiss expressed his unhappiness with Kohut, who was just then beginning to acquire a reputation for writing on narcissism, mainly because Kohut like others then in the psychoanalytic establishment refused to pay what Weiss thought was an adequate amount of attention to the contributions of Federn to modern ego psychology. In those days Heinz Hartmann's ideas about the ego were instead central to the so-called mainstream of analysis, even though Hartmann came from a much younger generation of analysts than Federn. By now fashions have changed again so that Hartmann's work gets cited much less today.[6]

In Italy Weiss had seen to it that there would be no restrictions on the practice of "lay," non-medical analysis, which is the way Freud had wanted it. Most of the members of Weiss's Society, though, were doctors; Servadio was an M.D., though Perrotti a Ph.D. Weiss thought that as long as an analyst who is a physician makes the initial diagnosis of the case, then a layperson could continue to undertake the treatment. Diagnoses in psychoanalytic psychotherapy can be a hazardous undertaking, and pigeonholing psychological clients remains more of an issue than even today's most psychopharmacologically inclined practitioners like to admit. It turned out that Weiss had once consulted with Freud about being sent a patient for analysis who was suffering from "absences," but in reality he had a tumor; the patient, who was a psychiatrist in Rome, had a wife who wrote directly to Freud as well as Weiss. Freud had not accurately detected the presence of an organic brain problem, and stood by his "earlier expectation of a good outcome."[7] The possibility that Freud had a tendency to overlook such possible physical afflictions could be worrisome to Freud himself, as well as to others who observed the rise of his new profession.

Although I did not inquire much about Weiss's personal life, his wife Wanda (1891-1967) had moved in the early 1950s to Berkeley, California, supposedly to get away from the Chicago climate. Weiss had met Wanda, originally from Pakrac in Croatia, while she was studying for her medical doctor's degree in Vienna. In 1915 she had been enrolled in Freud's course on psychoanalysis, and she started out as a pediatrician. Weiss and she became engaged during World War I and married shortly after she got her degree in 1917. Later in Chicago she was an excellent psychotherapist, although she took only a few cases and stayed pretty much to herself organizationally. Studs Terkel, later a Pulitzer Prize winner, was among her most notable patients.

Although she was reported to have been warm and sweet, Wanda's photos succeed in making her look primarily matronly. It is known that she objected to how hard Edoardo worked, and to other analysts at the Chicago Institute. Besides their two sons Emilio and Guido, young relatives of hers also lived with them in Rome; a niece from Croatia, Marianna, whose huge family was wiped out by the Ustashe[8], allied with the Nazis during World War II, became in 1949 a fully adopted daughter of Edoardo and Wanda. (Edoardo's youngest sister had married one of Wanda's brothers.) The couple retained a civilized European arrangement, marriage meant something different then than now, and they never quite acknowledged being emotionally separated; he lived with her over summers, while she was herself a practicing analyst. (Weiss had amidst his papers some copies of letters from Freud to Arthur Schnitzler, and Weiss thought it was because Wanda had been a friend of Schnitzler's first wife.) Weiss appeared to have a sad relation to Wanda, and he had a tendency to withdraw into himself.

Wanda had been trained in Rome by the Jungian Ernst Bernhard, from Germany but also Jewish, and Weiss traced his own difficulties with Anna Freud to his suspicion that she had heard stories from Margarete Ruben, an Italian analyst who had moved to London before World War II, about this "unorthodox" analysis of Wanda, and perhaps also about Weiss's own receptivity to Bernhard, who Weiss had invited to give lectures on dream interpretation to Weiss's Society. Wanda had first gone to Ruben, before Bernhard, for help, and Weiss had himself been interested in what Bernhard had to teach. During World War II Bernhard was protected by a fascist professor of oriental studies, and Bernhard later had contact with the film director Federico Fellini.

Weiss felt, based on what one of his students in Italy had told him, that Ruben had been malicious in what she reported about Weiss and his wife later in London, where Ruben was accorded the standing of becoming a "direct" member of the IPA.[9] At any rate Weiss put the central blame on Ruben for what he regarded as the unfortunate deterioration of his relationship with Anna Freud. (In medical school Weiss's fellow students had decided that he was incapable of developing two problems, becoming either phobic or paranoid.) Wanda's departure helped account for how Weiss's position in Chicago had to seem an isolated one; ambitious students at the Psychoanalytic Institute were going elsewhere for training, although he did seem to attract a group of non-medical psychologists. Thomas French, an old collaborator of Franz Alexander's, remained Weiss's closest analytic friend in Chicago, and when I knew him Weiss used to cook meals for French on Sundays.

Unlike those older American analysts like French, for example, who were without any personal contact with Freud and therefore knew him only from books, Weiss was always good with stories about Freud's mannerisms and personal characteristics: for example, how precise he was in his pronunciation, or how he played with a pencil on his desk by first tapping the tip, then the head, alternately. "Anna Freud does it exactly the same way," and Weiss felt she spoke publicly—without notes—just like her father did. Weiss thought that others too, even Tausk and Sandor Rado, who both were to have major difficulties in getting on with Freud, imitated him also in striking gestures, accents, words, and personal ways. Analysts had an almost comic identification with Freud that someone like Freud's daughter-in-law Esti thought worked against psychoanalysis in Vienna.[10] One has only to look at a photograph of Hartmann holding a cigar at a psychoanalytic meeting in Lucerne in 1934 to be strikingly reminded of a famous picture of Freud himself in that pose.[11] Weiss also remarked on how he remembered that Freud had had a ring with a green stone, and that he would play with it while giving pre-World War I lectures; others, along with Weiss, recalled how Freud could jangle with his watch-chain. Weiss recalled how Freud, after he fell ill from cancer, had commented about dogs that they were honest, one could trust their loves and hates, since they lacked the deceptions of humans.

In keeping with my own background, I was not just interested in the details of history, but sought for some generalizations that might be appropriate for a social scientist; and therefore I asked Weiss: *What were the clinical differences between patients in Italy and America*? After twenty-five years in the States, Weiss thought that while there were no central contrasts in symptomatology, Italians were "different from Americans—more intuitive, less strict, not so honest." Weiss saw more hysterical seizures in Italy than America; conversion symptoms, in which psychological conflicts were expressed somatically, were once common in Europe, but later relatively rare. Weiss reported that Freud had once observed of the clinical changes he had himself seen over the course of his career: "once there were fleas, and now after many years we do not find them any more."

Weiss emphasized that Freud himself was not interested in patients with "ego disturbances." Those Freud considered suitable for psychoanalytic treatment represented a much narrower range of clients than would now be considered accessible to psychotherapeutic intervention. On this score Federn, a generation younger, was ahead of Freud in taking a broader range of human beings into treatment. In a letter to Weiss Freud had rejected a paranoid patient for analysis[12]; even if Freud pioneered in understanding the characteristics of so-called primary process thinking, the primitive ways of expressing ourselves that come up so often in our dream life, that scarcely exhausted the problem of how to approach the clinical phenomena of psychosis. Like others who had been trained in European psychiatry Weiss knew how Freud's own neurological background left him clinically deficient. It was impossible for Weiss to get into many clinical discussions without his mentioning that Freud "did not understand psychotics," which led directly to Weiss's special appreciation for Federn's own exceptional contribution.

Federn had a lot of analysts in training with him who had worked outside the range of the classic neuroses, for example with the ego disturbances of juvenile delinquents. But as loyal as Federn was to Freud, Federn's own work went in another direction from that of Freud. Weiss thought that Federn's exceptional humanity made him more tolerant, and open to a wider range of patients, than Freud himself. "Federn did not want to make explicit his divergences from Freud, and be put in the same category as Adler or Jung." So Federn never organized anything like his own special school, but his distinctive approach had meant that someone like Aichhorn, and many others as well, had been much indebted to Federn's particular point of view. Erik H. Erikson could acknowledge his own indebtedness to Federn.[13] Weiss mentioned repeatedly a letter that Federn had sent him, about a month before he died, in which he said that his concepts had drifted further from Freud's own than Federn had ever realized.

I found that Weiss could be unreliable about certain aspects of the history of psychoanalysis with which he was not personally involved; and that he was apt to share in portions of the collective mythology that bound analysts together. For example, he viewed Freud's early collaborator Josef Breuer as a "coward" on the grounds that supposedly Breuer could not "face the realities of sexuality" in clinical encounters. But Weiss, who had not known Breuer, still seemed to think well of him, presumably based on Breuer's medical reputation in Vienna.

On the other hand, when Weiss could report something directly of his contact with Freud, it always seemed to me fresh and accurate. For example, as a native of Trieste Weiss had still served in the Austro-Hungarian army during World War I, and stopped off once to see Freud in Vienna dressed in the military uniform of a first lieutenant ("Oberazt"). Italy had entered the war in 1915 on the Allied side, breaking with the Central Powers, thanks to a plot hatched by the Prime Minister and King that amounted to a diplomatic revolution discrediting parliament.[14] Weiss got sent to the Austrian front because his pro-Italian convictions had been betrayed by someone from Trieste. By that time of Weiss's interview with Freud during World War I, Freud seemed to have given up the German nationalist sentiments he had had at the outset of the conflict, but he asked Weiss what he thought about the political prospects. Weiss had his views, and was patriotic about Italy, but basically he replied that he was a Jew and cared for the Jewish fate; therefore Weiss felt apart from the usual issues of politics. Freud was delighted at Weiss's attitude ("I like this much better!"), and shook hands. (When Freud was in Paris as a young man himself one can find him writing his fiancée about how he also felt as a Jew at the prospects of a Franco-Prussian war.[15])

I could not stay in Chicago any longer that April, but came back again in May, when Weiss and I had seven more interviewing sessions in the course of a week's time. Now Weiss trusted me in a relaxed and confidential way. *What was the analysis with Federn like*? It had begun on March 1, 1909. Like Freud, Federn—originally an internist—had his office at home in his apartment. The Max Oppenheimer portrait of Freud,[16] originally commissioned for Freud's oldest daughter Marthilda Hollitscher's wedding, in which Freud was beardless but wearing an English-trimmed mustache, hung next to the analytic couch. Weiss saw Federn six days a week, which was then the analytic custom, but Weiss did not think he had been merely "treated as a patient." Freud would have been too expensive for Weiss, since Freud then charged forty crowns an hour at time when a dollar was worth four crowns; a bachelor could then live "quite well" on two hundred crowns a month, and a nice suit cost about fifty or sixty crowns. Weiss, who would rather have been analyzed by Freud, paid Federn only twelve crowns an hour. When Weiss indicated to Federn his preference for Freud as an analyst, Federn removed from the consulting room the "disturbing" portrait of Freud.

Federn was still maintaining his practice in internal medicine in addition to doing analyses, and often his wife, then pregnant, would open the door, with her elder son at her side, for Weiss to enter. Federn also introduced his three-year-old daughter to Weiss. Such personal disclosures would not "be done now," Weiss held, but then he also pointed out that his status was not that of "just" a patient: he was a medical student with serious professional intentions.

Federn, who had been born in 1871, was then thirty-eight years old. He had gray eyes and was bald with a big, black beard, "very Jewish-looking." Weiss thought he resembled the great Viennese Zionist leader Theodor Herzl, but in later years members of the psychoanalytic movement would more likely compare his features to the Emperor Haile Selassie of Ethiopia. Federn was "very, very friendly" to Weiss, and Federn was cultured enough to make use of poetry and literature—Goethe, Schiller, Heine—in the analysis. (Besides Rilke and Broch, Elias Canetti, later a Nobel Prize winner, also came to Federn for help.) Sometimes Federn and Weiss would go together by taxi, after an analytic session, to get to the University. They remained close, "good friends," and exchanged a huge correspondence right up until Federn's death in 1950. Weiss felt there had been no artificial "distance" in his training analysis, and Weiss had remained a friend of Federn's son Ernst when I was doing this interviewing.

The analysis with Federn lasted a year and a half, and during the last two or three months Weiss saw him less frequently, about three times a week; such diminution of contact would have been a way of tapering off the analysis. At one difficult point they had gone together for a consultation with Freud, who saw Federn separately before Weiss; such informal supervision by Freud was evidently not unusual at that time. Weiss had a couple of analytic interviews with Freud after the conclusion of the treatment by Federn, to present his "achievements," but Weiss continued to consult with Federn informally as the years passed.

When I knew Weiss he saw Federn as far more humane than Freud. Although Federn was a great admirer of German culture, he did not like the strictness and discipline of the Germans. One of Federn's grandfathers had been a rabbi, but Federn married a Protestant and proceeded to baptize his children. (Ernst later spent years in Nazi concentration camps, while Walter sounds like an ambulatory schizophrenic, who Anna Freud had tried to treat as a child; Walter's problems could have stimulated Federn's interest in psychosis.) In the course of the analysis Federn revealed how fond he was of the Jesus figure; he thought children should be raised with an understanding of suffering. Weiss, who himself later married a Jewish woman, felt there were enough differences between himself and Federn that, although Weiss was devoted to Federn's memory, he still thought he could maintain the claim that he had never "identified" with Federn but had instead "retained his own identity."

Weiss's lack of differentiation with Federn meant that other analysts could be clearer about Federn's distinctive contributions than Weiss himself. The possibility of indoctrination in analysis has been touched on by different writers,[17] while the central place of lineage in the history of psychoanalysis has been more rarely talked about.[18] (Helene Deutsch, who as head of training in Vienna starting in the 1920s had had a slew of students at the Vienna Psychoanalytic Institute, could marvel to me how it had taken only one pupil of Federn's, Weiss, to have kept Federn's name alive. In New York City a private group of psychoanalytically trained psychologists, social workers and educators met as the Paul Federn Study Group from 1950 until 1961.)

Throughout the years 1908 to 1913 Weiss studied hard as a medical student; for exercise he took lessons fencing from the same master, Karpel, as Freud's own sons. Weiss had thought it was too soon to become a member of the Vienna Psychoanalytic Society. He had attended Freud's university lectures in the winter session of 1910; one needed his permission, on a written card, to be able to come, which was unusual; but in those days some people were inclined to attend for criticism and in order to make fun. Weiss was there (probably with Wanda) for Freud's first presentation of what became later his *Introductory Lectures on Psychoanalysis*; Weiss and Federn had unsuccessfully tried to copy down the initial lecture. This lecture series was the exception to Freud's usual practice of speaking without much preparation; each individual lecture was written out in the week preceding the Saturday when it was delivered.

Weiss always remembered how Freud had initially set out to discourage people from attending:

> Do not be annoyed…if I begin by treating you in the same way as… neurotic patients. I seriously advise you not to join my audience a second time. To support this advice, I will explain to you how incomplete any instruction in psychoanalysis must necessarily be and what difficulties stand in the way of your forming a judgment of your own about it. I will show you how the whole trend of your previous education and all your habits of thought are inevitably bound to make you into opponents of psychoanalysis, and how much you would have to overcome in yourselves in order to get the better of this instinctive opposition. I cannot, of course, foretell how much understanding of psychoanalysis you will obtain from the information I give you, but I can promise you this: that by listening to it you will not have learnt how to set about a psychoanalytic investigation or how to carry a treatment through. If, however, there should actually turn out to be one of you who did not feel satisfied by a fleeting acquaintance with psychoanalysis, but was inclined to enter into a permanent relationship with it, I should not merely dissuade him from doing so but actively warn him against it. As things stand at present, such a choice of profession would ruin any chance he might have of success at a University, and, if he started in life as a practicing physician, he would find himself in a society which did not understand his efforts, which regarded him with distrust and hostility, and unleashed upon him all the evil spirits lurking within it. And the phenomena accompanying the war that is now raging in Europe will perhaps give you some notion of what legions of these evil spirits there may be.
>
> Nevertheless, there are quite a number of people for whom, in spite of these inconveniences, something that promises to bring them a fresh piece of knowledge still has its attractions. If a few of you should be of this sort and in spite of my warnings appear here again for my next lecture, you will be welcome.[19]

Weiss himself did not become notably successful as a lecturer. One Chicago student thought Weiss had a version of "stage fright"; he would be very anxious before an audience, and could seem like a different person in public. While overwhelmed by anxiety he became authoritative-seeming. Perhaps Weiss was a bit jealous of how well Kohut succeeded as a speaker. If Weiss had his own lecturing handicap, so did Federn, who was apt to be publicly confused. Weiss could, nonetheless, describe just how Freud himself was uniquely eloquent and powerful in his own lectures. He had a way of arguing by means of inventing possible points of opposition to himself, and then he would demonstrate his own counter-arguments.

A couple of years before Freud's presentation of his *Introductory Lectures*, Tausk had in 1913 suggested that Weiss join the Vienna Psychoanalytic Society, and when asked about it Federn said "of course!" Weiss then went to see Freud to ask if he could become a member before getting his M.D. in 1914, and Freud was delighted at the idea. At that time if someone were known to Freud the delivery of a paper before the Society was enough to secure such acceptance. So Weiss gave a talk on the forgetting of names, and was unanimously elected.[20] The question of allowing women to become full members had been hotly enough contested in 1910, despite Freud's personally endorsing the idea, that he spoke some words then about the need to move cautiously in the future[21]; Freud had proceeded anyway to award women status in his movement that was unusual for the time. After Weiss himself joined he regularly went to Wednesday evening meetings of the Society.

Weiss was full of material for me about the pre-World War I medical scene in Vienna. He studied both neurology and psychiatry, as did his friend Tausk, although Freud himself was primarily trained as a neurologist. Weiss made sure that he worked at the Psychiatric Clinic of Julius Wagner von Jauregg, and took his psychiatric examinations under him.[22] Freud, although he and Wagner respected each other, remained an outsider to Viennese psychiatry. It had to be impressive to Weiss that Freud gave his lectures, before twenty or thirty people, in the same room that Wagner-Jauregg taught in.

But at a café discussion after a meeting of the Vienna Society Weiss heard about an early case of Freud's that illustrated the difference between neurosis and psychosis, a distinction Freud at first had been reluctant to make since Freud had hopes that psychoanalysis could ultimately conquer all human ills. In that period Freud still used the term "narcissistic neuroses" to gloss over the differences between neurosis and psychosis, so that he did not clarify the large conceptual point in print until the 1920s. (Jung, a psychiatrist, had been presciently insistent on the importance of distinguishing between neurosis and psychosis.) According to Weiss, Freud thought that if "analysis could solve all the problems of the world he would have been happy." (Hartmann too summarized Wagner's objections to Freud in terms of his over-ambitiousness.) Unquestionably Freud before World War I was defining "neurosis" far more broadly than he would have later on.

In this early case illustration, one that Weiss heard about from Freud so informally, a patient who had come for treatment suffering from an agoraphobic symptom had been successfully "cured" hypnotically after only a few weeks. "After a few days," however, the woman showed "signs of acute schizophrenia." Freud then visited the patient, hypnotized her again, this time to reintroduce the agoraphobia, and thereby overcame the schizophrenia. "For years thereafter the patient wrote to him expressing her great gratitude."[23] Weiss thought that the case demonstrated that many neuroses can be a defense against a psychotic breakdown. (Weiss's conclusion would have parallels to Melanie Klein's contention about the close relationship of psychosis to normality, and when I later interviewed Donald Winnicott in London he wanted to know more about this case, after I brought it up, that had so interested Weiss.[24])

A summary of a 1936 paper of Weiss's, entitled "The Early Diagnosis of Psychoses in Analysands," was reported in *The International Journal of Psychoanalysis*, and gives a snapshot of Weiss's characteristic and enduring convictions:

> A latent psychosis in an analysand may be diagnosed from certain signs, mental attitudes and psychic processes, even before symptoms occur which the psychiatrist knows to be typically psychotic. Early diagnosis of a latent psychosis is important, because psychotics must be treated differently from neurotics. In practice the two principal psychoses concerning us are paranoia and schizophrenia.
>
> It sometimes happens that the clinical picture of a neurosis conceals a psychosis; the neurosis then represents either a manifest facade or a superstructure of the psychosis. (It is true that there are also mixed cases: genuine neurotic symptoms in psychotics and psychotic characteristics in neurotics.) The frequent experience that, as the revealing work of analysis went on, a manifest neurosis was demolished only to be replaced by a psychosis led the author to conclude that the latter may be subjected to a process analogous to repression, a "defense" being set up against it by means of the substitution of a neurotic condition.
>
> When neurotic symptoms are also present, they are taken into the service of the process of secondary elaboration which we see at work in delusions, in the same way as factors belonging to the external world are also utilized.[25]

When Weiss had gone back to Trieste at the end of World War I to start practicing analysis, he thought he had already become well acquainted with the psychoses. Federn had taught that providing the therapist knows enough to listen, psychotics can be self-healing; but that an analyst should not "interpret the transference in the treatment of psychotic patients."[26] Weiss was a physician at a psychiatric hospital in Trieste, and also in private practice as a Freudian. The city had only a couple of hundred thousand citizens, and Weiss found that he did not have enough patients; he tried and failed to get an analytic group around him started. A paradox about numbers has always existed for analysts: where an analyst works alone there is going to be more trouble earning a livelihood, while with a hundred analysts in a city there are likely to be many more referrals.

Following World War I Weiss started to publish his findings, both in medical and psychoanalytic journals. He was at the time especially interested in the problem of bronchial asthma, which he interpreted as a form of suppressed crying for the mother. Mothers were then still relatively little written about in the analytic literature, until thinkers like Otto Rank, Georg Groddeck, Sandor Ferenczi, Helene Deutsch, and Melanie Klein helped put motherhood on the map for analysts. Later the Chicago Institute under Alexander would interpret many psychosomatic symptoms as a sign of the suppression of talking and confession. Even today scientists continue to study the mind-body problem, and for example the way chronic stress can affect the immune system.

Weiss then attended every international meeting of psychoanalysis, although by the time I knew him he went to none of them. In 1931 he had moved from Trieste to Rome. Earlier he had

> resigned from his job at the [Provincial Psychiatric] Hospital in 1927…as he would not agree to Italianize his surname and join the Fascist party. The regulations concerning public employment had become very strict in Italy after 1926: no one could any longer be employed by the State without being a member of the Fascist party.[27]

At the beginning in Rome Weiss had a hard time establishing his practice. A psychologist moderately favorable to Freud, Professor Sante de Sanctis, had promised to send Weiss patients in Rome, but nothing came of them; apparently de Sanctis was "lukewarm" toward psychoanalysis, in that he preferred the term "subconscious" to "unconscious," and he criticized Freud for having "exaggerated" the role of sexuality. Apparently at this point, during Weiss's early days struggling to live in Rome, he wrote a worried letter to Freud, which elicited such a striking lack of sympathy on Freud's part that although Emilio Weiss, Weiss's older son, remembered his father as having been terribly disappointed at having received it, the letter has not survived.

Although it must have taken an extraordinary act to do away with something so sacred to Weiss as a Freud letter, it seems that Weiss must have destroyed it. The issue of the destruction of Freud letters has scarcely ever been examined; we know that Freud wrote his fiancée in 1885 about how Freud anticipated misleading future biographers by discarding all sorts of early papers[28], and before leaving Vienna in 1938 another large batch of Freudiana got thrown out. In addition, it now can be established that, like Weiss, Rado destroyed at least some Freud letters to him, as also did Brill.

By 1932 Weiss had analyzed and trained a couple of professional allies, Servadio and Perrotti, and with them he re-founded the Italian Psychoanalytic Society that Levi-Bianchini had supposedly started earlier. Servadio and Perrotti had so many disagreements that Weiss spoke to me of the existence of two Italian psychoanalytic groups. Weiss had also analyzed Perrotti's brother-in-law, Raffaele Merloni, a Gentile and Social Democrat who was interested in law, as he became a practicing analyst. Cesare Musatti, a psychologist who was not analyzed, joined them from Padua. Israele Zolli had been a rabbi in Trieste, and since he was scientifically minded and interested in symbolism, Weiss became very close to him; later he became Grand Rabbi in Rome, but then converted to Catholicism.

Freud personally ensured that for the first time the Italian group would win the official backing of the International Psychoanalytic Association (IPA). In Rome they published a review, *Rivista di Psicanalisi*, and Weiss gave some lectures; even though evidently Mussolini would have liked the new psychoanalytic institute to continue, the journal Weiss started lasted only a couple of years. A couple of church leaders seem to have been responsible for the suppression of psychoanalytic writings; Weiss wrote to Federn that "it is in order to safeguard morality that they have not allowed me to go on publishing the journal!" Psychoanalysis's so called pansexualism was deemed a source of immorality, and "champions of the Fascist cause...criticized 'degenerate' psychoanalysis, emphasizing in frequently grotesque tones the incompatible elements of two completely opposite theories of man."[29]

The full force of the anti-Semitic laws in Italy finally drove Weiss and his immediate family to emigrate. Italy, whose Jewish population made up approximately one-tenth of the total population, had had virtually no anti-Semitism; Jews had held high posts in various governmental ministries, and many Italians were appalled by Hitler's approach to the Jewish question. Jewish communities had long existed, besides in Trieste, also in Florence, Livorno, Genoa, and Rome. So Mussolini's new laws came as a shock.[30]

A full Weiss family council met to decide how they should each proceed. Edoardo and Emilio (endangered by the possibility of being drafted) sailed from Naples in January 1939. And Wanda, concerned about the fate of various members of her own family, later left with Guido from Naples too in October. (Levi-Bianchini, "an adherent of the Fascist party,"[31] was the rare Jew in the psychoanalytic Society who remained in Italy; Servadio, for example, went to India until the war was over.)

As important as I thought it was to dwell on Weiss's experiences in Italy, I also wanted to direct my questioning in such a way as to elicit information about the great battles in analysis during Freud's lifetime. It turned out that he did not know much at first hand about them. He was not present for the quarrel over Adler within the Vienna Society, at which time Federn had sided with Freud against Adler. But the split between Freud and Jung seemed "a shame" to Weiss, and he regretted that Jung's works were on the psychoanalytic church's "Index" of forbidden books. (So were those by Rank; but then Weiss also thought that these "deviants" had "rejected" in Freud "many things which are true." Weiss had three or four hours of consultation with Rank, who would not accept payment.) Weiss knew a bit about Wilhelm Stekel, since he saw him after Stekel had left the Vienna Psychoanalytic Society; he had once sent Weiss an impotent young man for treatment on the patient's way to Palestine in 1923-24. To Weiss, Stekel was not very reliable, and Weiss said he heard that Stekel could be "sexual with patients." In the case of the young man whom Stekel had sent to him in 1923, Stekel had examined the patient's penis to see if he could have an erection or not, even though "no analyst would have done such a thing." Once in 1922 Weiss wrote Freud about a psychiatrist patient who admired Stekel's writings, and Freud replied that "it was a worrisome sign of poor judgment and of perverted taste...."[32] (Stekel met Svevo, and therefore Stekel rather than Weiss could have been the model for Svevo's fictional psychoanalyst.[33])

Stekel might have been highly "imaginative" but he was not adequately scientific. His clinical cases could not be relied upon; even though Stekel always continued to admire Freud, according to Weiss the founder of psychoanalysis did not like "people who lacked an ethical or moral character." Yet Weiss agreed, when I reminded him of the point, that no matter how insistent Freud could be on uprightness, he could still be extraordinarily gullible. Weiss thought that "one of Freud's pronounced traits was his immediate liking for anyone who was interested in psychoanalysis or was its protagonist, and because of it he occasionally grossly misjudged people."

Weiss was not shy about discussing an apparently different character trait of Freud's, which he discussed under the category of what Weiss called Freud's "intolerance." Yet it was precisely Freud's high expectations about people that could lead directly to his later bitter disappointments. Both Weiss and Freud considered the group of analysts "like a family," defining that term in its extended European meaning, and if anyone did not obey the rules he would be ousted. Federn was personally handicapped in his writing by the conflict between trying to remain loyal to Freud and still being able to express his own psychological vision. Federn did not want to show any signs of his disagreements with Freud. When I asked Weiss what one could not doubt, and still stay on as an analyst, Weiss quickly listed four central concepts of Freud's that were beyond discussion: dreams as wish-fulfillment, the instinct theory, the Oedipus complex, and the castration complex. About Weiss's own conceptual contributions to psychoanalysis I thought Weiss rather tended to confuse words with things, although it may have been natural authorial vanity.

Although Weiss himself had little personal difficulty staying loyal to these central Freudian tenets of belief that he itemized, at least while Freud was still alive, Weiss did mind that Freud seemed only to have quoted students who applied his main concepts, or developed them along the lines he could approve of. Anna Freud too, in her famous *The Ego and Mechanisms of Defence*, was similarly peculiar in how she made her acknowledgements. Federn was so offended by her lack of appreciation for his own ego psychology that according to Weiss he did "not talk to her for a couple of months" after the appearance of her 1936 book. By those days Federn, as Vice President of the Vienna Society, was chairing all its meetings in Freud's absence. To Weiss, Anna was one of those who wrote, even though in the new area of child analysis, primarily to "confirm" Freud.

Notes

1. Roazen, *Freud and His Followers* (New York: Alfred A. Knopf, 1975), pp. 211-22.
2. See "The Psychopathology of Everyday Life," *Standard Edition*, Vol. 6 (London: The Hogarth Press, 1953-74), p. 169; "Analysis of a Phobia in a Five-Year Old Boy," *Standard Edition*, Vol. 10, p. 16; "On Narcissism," *Standard Edition*, Vol. 14, p. 82; "Civilization and Its Discontents," *Standard Edition*, Vol. 21, p. 75.
3. Oskar Pfister, "The Illusion of a Future: A Friendly Disagreement with Prof. Sigmund Freud," ed. by Paul Roazen and with an introduction, *International Journal of Psychoanalysis*, Vol. 74 (June 1993), pp. 557-79.
4. *Letters of Sigmund Freud to Eduard Silberstein 1871-1881*, edited by Walter Boehlich, translated by Arnold J. Pomerans (Cambridge, MA: Harvard University Press, 1990), pp. 70-71.
5. Edoardo Weiss, *Sigmund Freud as a Consultant, Recollections of a Pioneer in Psychoanalysis*, with an Introduction by Martin Grotjahn (New York: Intercontinental Medical Book Corporation, 1970; New Brunswick, NJ: Transaction Publishers, 1991), p. 69.
6. *The Hartmann Era*, ed. Martin S. Bergmann (New York: Other Press, 2000).
7. Weiss, *Sigmund Freud as a Consultant*, pp. 38-39.
8. Robert D. Kaplan, *Balkan Ghosts* (New York: Vintage, 1994).
9. But see two unpublished 1981 memorial tributes to Grete Ruben when she died in Los Angeles: one by Miriam Williams, the other by Dr. Heiman Van Dam.
10. Paul Roazen, *Meeting Freud's Family* (Amherst: University of Massachusetts Press, 1993), p. 159.
11. *Die Freudianer: Fotografien von Tim N. Gidal* (Munich and Vienna: Verlag Internationale Psychoanalyse, 1990), No. 30.
12. Weiss, *Sigmund Freud as a Consultant*, pp. 57-58.
13. Erik H. Erikson, *Identity: Youth and Crisis* (New York: W.W. Norton, 1968), pp. 9, 209; Erik H. Erikson, *Life History and the Historical Moment* (New York: W.W. Norton, 1975), p. 37.

14. Denis Mack Smith, *Modern Italy: A Political History* (Ann Arbor: University of Michigan Press, 1997), pp. 262, 267.
15. *Letters of Sigmund Freud*, ed. Ernst Freud (London: Hogarth Press, 1961), p. 203.
16. Roazen, *Meeting Freud's Family*, pp. 130-31.
17. Robert Jay Lifton, *Thought Reform and the Psychology of Totalism: A Study of "Brainwashing" in China* (New York: W.W. Norton, 1963), pp. 446-49. And see Robert Hinshelwood, *Therapy Or Coercion: Does Psychoanalysis Differ from Brainwashing?* (London: Karnac Books, 1997).
18. Ernst Falzeder, "The Threads of Psychoanalytic Filiations or Psychoanalysis Taking Effect," in *100 Years of Psychoanalysis*, ed. André Haynal and Ernst Falzeder (London: Karnac [Books] Ltd.,1994), pp.169-94. See also Paul Roazen, "Charles Rycroft and the Theme of Ablation," *British Journal of Psychotherapy*, Vol. 18, No. 2 (2001).
19. Weiss, *Sigmund Freud as a Consultant*, p.6; "The Introductory Lectures on Psychoanalysis," *Standard Edition*, Vol. 15, pp. 15-16.
20. *Minutes of the Vienna Psychoanalytic Society*, Vol. 4: *1912-1918*, ed. Herman Nunberg and Ernst Federn, translated by M. Nunberg in collaboration with Harold Collins (New York: International Universities Press, 1975), pp. 198-201
21. *Minutes of the Vienna Psychoanalytic Society*, Vol. 2: *1908-1910*, ed. Herman Nunberg and Ernst Federn, translated by M. Nunberg (New York: International Universities Press, 1967), p. 477.
22. Paul Roazen, "Psychoanalysis's Cotton Mather: Review of Eissler, *Freud As An Expert Witness*," *Contemporary Psychology*, Vol. 33, No. 3 (March 1988), pp. 213-14. Also in Roazen, *Cultural Foundations of Political Psychology* (New Brunswick, NJ: Transaction Publishers, 2003), pp. 160-161.
23. Edoardo Weiss, *Agoraphobia in the Light of Ego Psychology* (New York: Grune and Stratton, 1964), p. 6.
24. Roazen, *The Historiography of Psychoanalysis* (New Brunswick, NJ: Transaction Publishers, 2000), p. 182.
25. *International Journal of Psychoanalysis*, Vol. 17 (1937), p. 78.
26. Weiss, *Sigmund Freud as a Consultant*, p 42.
27. A. M. Accerboni, "Psychoanalysis and Fascism, Two Incompatible Approaches: The Difficult Role of Edoardo Weiss," *Review of the International History of Psychoanalysis*, Vol. 1 (1988), pp. 225-240.
28. Roazen, *The Historiography of Psychoanalysis*, p. 2.
29. Accerboni, "Psychoanalysis and Fascism."
30. Meir Michaelis, *Mussolini and the Jews: German-Italian Relations and the Jewish Question in Italy* (Oxford: Clarendon Press, 1978).
31. *The Complete Correspondence of Sigmund Freud and Karl Abraham* (London: Karmac, 2002), p. 284.
32. Weiss, *Sigmund Freud as a Consultant*, p. 39.
33. Elizabeth Mahler-Schächter, "Svevo, Trieste, and the Vienna Circle: Zeno's Analyst Analysed," *European Studies Review*, vol. 12, no. 1 (Jan. 1982).

6

An Interview with Kurt Eissler

After we had gotten to know each other well enough, Weiss entrusted me with some written material in his possession. In 1952, Kurt R. Eissler, on behalf of the Freud Archives in New York City, tape-recorded an interview with Weiss; and he afterwards had sent Weiss a copy of the manuscript so Weiss could check it over. In 1965, when I was seeing Weiss myself, the manuscript had been already locked up by Eissler in behalf of the Freud Archives in the Sigmund Freud Collection at the Library of Congress in Washington, D.C. until the year 2057. Although Eissler regularly had an excessively cautious conception of what the public could safely be allowed to learn about Freud, no other interview that he conducted was sealed up by him longer than the one with Weiss.

Yet the text itself neither shows Eissler in any great disagreement with anything that Weiss has to say to him, as Eissler regularly relied only on free associations in his interviews,[1] nor is there much there on Weiss's part that could be considered terribly radical or subversive. The only damage by releasing it immediately might have been to idealized conceptions of what Freud was like. Even Freud's last will in England was locked up in those days until the year 2007, although it had been since 1939 a public document available through Somerset House in London; I arranged for the 1990 publication of that will precisely because it seemed to me an example of nonsensical secrecy.[2] By the time of Weiss's death he had arranged for the interview he gave to Eissler to be freely available amidst Weiss's own papers that he had left at the Library of Congress. Eissler's making the Freud Archives the principal donor to the Sigmund Freud Collection at the Library meant that Eissler could control the release dates on what he himself deposited there, whatever the wishes of someone like Weiss might have been.[3] Other examples of such discrepancies between Eissler's Freud Collection and the will of donors to him could also be pointed out.

Now Weiss had known Eissler originally in Chicago, where Eissler had once practiced before moving to New York City. Weiss would have realized what a critic of Franz Alexander's work Eissler was, and perhaps surmised the power Eissler had acquired within the international psychoanalytic hierarchy. And Weiss might have felt, given his own distant relation with the Chicago analysts, reluctant about unnecessarily ruffling Eissler's orthodox psychoanalytic feathers. Someone as organizationally ambitious as Kohut went to Eissler's wife Ruth for Kohut's own analysis. According to Kohut's biographer, the Eisslers had a "luxurious apartment" in Chicago. Kohut was in 1946 establishing himself quickly "as an earnest Freudian, applauding the orthodox teaching of Eduardo Weiss and quietly questioning Theresa Benedek's significant departures from classical technique."[4]

While I was seeing Weiss, Benedek was one of the local analyst's I made sure also to interview. I found then nothing very striking about her "departures," since I felt her to be a charming Hungarian who embodied the kind of cultured flexibility of other pioneering continental analysts. I also knew she was on particularly good terms with Helene Deutsch, and they both had specialized on the topic of the nature of female psychology.

Weiss had told Eissler at the outset of his interview how Freud's theories had first affected Weiss's own thinking.

> I understood that we have in ourselves some resonance box, or resounding board, as it were, so that when we see something, or we experience something, all the past memories give their overtones to our experiences. I explained this through unconscious associations, as everybody could. And then I read the Traumdeutung [*The Interpretation of Dreams*] and I saw that there was much more to it than only unconscious associations, namely that Freud had discovered a complicated psychological mechanism which we had ignored previously. And besides, I myself had some neurotic disturbance, *not* very severe, some inhibition; and I was a little timid in speaking among people, and so I wondered whether it would not be a good idea to become acquainted with this discipline.[5]

Weiss went on to explain to Eissler exactly how he had happened to see Freud in 1908. And Eissler responded to Weiss: "Oh, you met Freud?"[6] Now this innocuous-seeming interviewing ploy of Eissler's seems to me representative of a Uriah Heep-like characteristic of Eissler. Of course he had to have known, if only from the Freud letters that Weiss had shown Eissler, that Weiss had "met" Freud. As Weiss rather enjoyed telling me, Eissler had in Vienna himself never set eyes on Freud, even though in establishing the Freud Archives Eissler went around with a tape recorder interviewing people he could find who had known Freud.

When I myself eventually had my only interview with Eissler in April 1967, Eissler was fully cooperative, but it was relatively late in my interviewing and I felt pretty detached from what he told me. Originally Eissler had in a 1963 letter tried to discourage me from the idea that early analysts would cooperate with being interviewed as I proposed; then, having heard a good deal about me from Helene Deutsch, he was receptive to my work. But I already felt that Eissler was unable to appreciate the full significance of any of the personal memories about Freud I had myself collected, for example in reconsidering the great conflicts Freud had had with people like Jung, Adler, and Rank. Eissler was partisanly engaged in the standard mythology surrounding Freud's life, a series of stories that Freud himself had set going, and at the time I saw Eissler I made note to myself of Eissler's commitment to the conventional legend weaving. But Eissler himself seemed courtly and almost obsequious toward me; the same day that I saw Eissler I happened to be also interviewing a Viennese child analyst, Berta Bornstein, in New York City, and Eissler was so solicitous as to have telephoned her before I arrived to be sure I had gotten there safely. Nothing I myself experienced personally of Eissler, however, adequately prepared me for the vengeful fury of his responses to my publication *Brother Animal: The Story of Freud and Tausk* in 1969.[7] Eissler pursued me in print for almost thirty years because of what he took to be the crimes of my interpretations. While Anna Freud was alive he was proceeding with her cooperation against me, and for a time even Helene Deutsch allied herself with Eissler. After he had his own subsequent falling out with Helene Deutsch, he was reported to have been most unhappy at her appointing me to write her authorized biography. Even at the conclusion of the last book he ever published he was again accusing me of having alleged that Freud had "murdered" Tausk.[8] Weiss had been a classmate of Tausk's at medical school in Vienna, even though Tausk was much older and already established as a member of the Vienna Society.

Weiss remained always struck by Freud's having been temporarily clean-shaven when Weiss first met him in 1908; Freud was briefly then wearing "an English trimmed mustache." "It was only recently that he did not wear a beard. He wrote, I think in some book…, that when he had mixed hair, white-gray-black, he didn't like it. But it was only for a short time that he was beardless." Weiss knew that there was that oil painting of Freud from that period by Oppenheimer which has already been mentioned; it later hung at the New York Psychoanalytic Society. Weiss wanted to know if Eissler had seen it, and it turned out that Federn had once shown it to Eissler.

At the hundredth anniversary of Freud's birth in 1856 the painting was included among other Freud memorabilia at an exhibition in New York City, and Weiss had told me how he had spotted the incorrect date of 1909, when Weiss could be certain it had been done in late 1908. Federn had arranged for the painting to be done in honor of Freud's oldest daughter Mathilda's impending marriage, but that she had not liked it and it got returned to Federn.[9]

Weiss remained shocked, as he told me but not Eissler, that at that 1956 meeting Ernest Jones had alleged of a slight tear in the painting that that was where Federn had supposedly shot at Freud before finally killing himself in 1950. Federn's wife had predeceased him, he faced a second operation for cancer, and did not want to face another post-operative breakdown. (The distinguished analyst Bertram Lewin was present with Weiss and Jones on the occasion of the story about the tear in the painting, and according to Weiss Lewin wrote him afterwards that he had not believed Jones's story—but Lewin had failed to sign the letter to Weiss, as if, according to Weiss, Lewin had wanted to remove himself as much as possible from Jones's sort of malice. The painting was actually in storage at the time of Federn's death.[10]) The reader will remember how when Weiss had mentioned in his analysis how he would have preferred to be analyzed by Freud, instead of Federn, Federn had had the painting which hung then on the wall on the right side of the analytic couch, removed from his office. Federn's analytic fees were far lower than Freud's, and more affordable for Weiss.

Right from the outset Weiss had been taken by Freud.

> I was quite enthused about this man who made such an *overwhelming* impression on me, by his clear and penetrating eyes, the friendliness of his manner, his very evident goodness, and his warmth. I immediately had the feeling that I was before a genius, a quite outstanding personality. And I had the impression that he enjoyed speaking with me. When I was about to leave, he said: "Why are you in such a hurry?" I think that he liked meeting somebody from Trieste...And he shook hands in a very cordial way, raising his arm in a gesture of warmth....[11]

At one point in the analysis with Federn that Freud had recommended, not because he thought that Weiss "urgently" had need of it but because Freud approved of analysis for "everyone interested in becoming an analyst," Weiss had gone with Federn back to Freud for a consultation about Weiss's analytic progress. Freud felt that in the course of Weiss's analysis some symptoms that had not been so apparent might have become "more acute." Weiss reported to Eissler that "in the course of analysis I had experienced some slight anxiety states, in connection with some material that came up, and Freud told me that this was a common occurrence in the analytic process."[12]

After Weiss terminated the analysis, he was permitted in 1910 to attend the lectures by Freud at the university. While already a student Weiss had started to analyze someone with a " very severe obsessional neurosis," and because Weiss had "great difficulties with the patient" he decided to consult Freud. In hindsight Weiss thought it was really a case of schizophrenia. Although Eissler wanted the patient's name, Weiss momentarily hesitated to provide that information, but Eissler wanted to know if he could have that information so he could try to track him down. Weiss remarked of the patient that he was "one of the most *severe* compulsive neuroses that I have ever seen." In a consultation Weiss had with Freud, the patient indicated that he had not wanted to come to his analytical hours before the customary afternoon coffee. "And Freud laughingly asked, 'Are you afraid you may eat Dr. Weiss up.' The patient had to have his stomach full before he could come to the hour. So this was an allusion in a very subtle way to his oral aggression!"[13]

Tausk, to repeat, had been the one who in 1913 first asked Weiss why he did not apply for membership in the Vienna Society. Federn agreed with the idea: "in those days, if a person was known to Freud, the presentation of a paper before the Society was sufficient to enable him to be accepted as a member."[14] Weiss had had the chance to see Freud not only in consultations, in his lectures at the University and in the meetings of the Vienna Society, but also "quite privately in the Café Bauer,"[15] close to the Burgtheater, for informal gatherings. Weiss mentioned to Eissler how Otto Rank in particular "was always *quite* close to Freud, and how much he admired him and how much he wished to be useful to him...." At this point Weiss hesitated whether he should proceed, but Eissler encouraged Weiss to go on. Rank was, according to Weiss, in those early days "very dependently attached to Freud. He was so glad when he could fill Freud's water glass or light his cigar."[16]

Weiss immediately went on to talk more about Tausk, although Weiss hesitated about whether he had "the right to reveal such intimate" matters. When Weiss asked Eissler whether the interview would get read by others, Eissler answered: "In a hundred years....Nobody will read it until then, if anyone reads it at all; but I think it is *so* important" that Weiss pursue his thoughts.[17] Weiss therefore continued: "Tausk revealed his ambivalence toward Freud."[18] (Although psychoanalytic doctrine teaches that divided feelings are inevitable in all important human relations, only toward Freud himself would orthodoxy command that such emotions be considered impermissible.) I had to conclude that Weiss was incredibly trusting not to suspect that whatever he told Eissler about Freud, even if it were locked up for over a hundred years, would first of all get straight from Eissler to Anna Freud in London. (In her own first interview with me she had waxed far more enthusiastic about Eissler's writings on her father than on Jones's.)

According to Weiss Tausk thought that Freud had not treated him "well." Tausk considered that he had made some important psychological findings before Freud; for example, about the importance of narcissistic wounds in causing repression. Creative writers may have always known, for example, that wounded vanity can produce an amnesia, but early psychoanalysis did not assign the ego such a critical role in forgetfulness. In Tausk's view, however, Freud would not agree to Tausk's publishing an insight of his first. For, "in Tausk's opinion, Freud wanted to publish his findings in the way in which he had discovered them personally and in the specific connections in which he had discovered them. Tausk objected to this because it prevented him from asserting himself in an original manner."[19] (Eissler gained in his sealed files an independent account by another analyst, Ludwig Jekels, of why Freud had been stand-offish in refusing to analyze Tausk, which would be confirmed to me by other early analysts. Jekels had quoted Freud as having declared about Tausk: "He is going to kill me!"[20] Yet when I later publicized the story of all the various complicated difficulties between Freud and Tausk, Eissler somehow came to pretend that any such struggle was "fictitious."[21])

Weiss had gone to say that he remembered

> a remark about Freud which Tausk made to me privately and about which I believe he was wrong. In his opinion Freud suffered from a slight paranoic trait, because he always had a close friend whom he later dropped, becoming then that person's enemy and choosing a new friend. Probably this was a projection by Tausk of his own traits.[22]

Weiss evidently had forgotten a notable passage in Freud's *The Interpretation of Dreams* in which he had described just such a trait in himself, but attributed it to a childhood relationship with a nephew of his, which "had become the source of all my friendships and all my hatreds."

> My emotional life has always insisted that I should have an intimate friend and a hated enemy. I have always been able to provide myself afresh with both, and it has not infrequently happened that the ideal situation of childhood has been so completely reproduced that friend and enemy have come together in a single individual—though not, of course, both at once or with constant oscillations, as may have been the case in my early childhood.[23]

It would be characteristic of Freud to put in his version of his childhood a problem that had beset him also in adulthood. Weiss mentioned with me not just Freud's fallings out with Adler and Jung, but the difficulties with Ferenczi, Karl Abraham, and Eugen Bleuler.

Weiss was insistent with Eissler about Freud's "great honesty and his open-mindedness," and provided concrete illustrations:

> Freud told everyone: Whoever feels the urge to investigate some phenomenon should go ahead and do so, whatever the subject might be. I happened to have in treatment later on, in Trieste, two patients who had been analyzed previously for a short time by Freud. And through them I learned something of Freud's attitudes. In one case Freud told the patient: Suppose you have the idea that you can discover something from the lines of the hand. Don't be hindered by preconceived ideas. Go ahead and investigate! But you must consider whether your belief might be due to some unconscious motive which you don't understand, or whether the interest is genuine. At any rate, we have to feel free to investigate whatever fields interest us; there are so many things between heaven and earth...of which we are completely ignorant.[24]

Although Weiss was convinced of Freud's "great honesty, his freedom of mind," Weiss also pointed out to Eissler

> Another characteristic of his which I want to mention: the fact that he was very jealous with respect to his creation—analysis. He was greatly disturbed when analysis was misconstrued and his concepts distorted. He became angry if someone distorted his statements even in good faith. On the other hand, he felt very grateful to all who accepted analysis, and he quoted very willingly any publication expounding new applications or new confirmations of what he himself had originally discovered. Conversely, if someone arrived at a view which was at variance with what he himself taught, he was reluctant to accept it.[25]

One has to appreciate the pious religiosity of someone like Eissler to follow how offended he could have been by Weiss's cautiously worded characterizations of Freud.

Weiss chose an example bearing on the historiography of psychoanalysis that came up in his own correspondence with Freud. In a 1914 paper of Freud's he criticized Adler's concept of "masculine protest," preferring instead to trace the clinical phenomena to the castration complex, or the rebellion against being castrated; Freud had then argued, against Adler, that there are cases in which no castration complex can be found, and that then the phenomena would be outside the range of Adler's whole approach.

When Weiss in 1926 wrote Freud asking about this passage, trying to understand what Freud might have meant, he said in reply that he felt put "in an embarrassing position. I no longer recollect what it was I had in mind at the time. Today, it is true, I would not name any neurosis in which this complex is not to be met with, and in any case I should not have written the sentence today."[26] Weiss thought that "from the context of his original statement it is quite evident that he had simply looked for a point against Adler, you know! In my opinion all the dissidents would have remained in his group if Freud had been a little more tolerant toward divergent ideas." This was a line of reasoning Eissler would never accept, though he raised no objections to Weiss in his presence, who continued: "I really think that he was not very tolerant. Not out of ill-faith, of course! But he had a protective attitude toward his own creation, his own child, of which he was very jealous."[27] Weiss cited Federn in this connection, as someone who was "*very* loyal and very much attached to Freud." Federn

> mentioned that if some author brought out completely new views, at variance with Freud's own theories, Freud didn't like to mention them too much. Often, however, Freud would be stimulated to think about these views and eventually to express them in a clearer way in connection with his own analytical constructions. He didn't discard these ideas...But he had to work them through and elaborate upon them in his own mind until he succeeded in assimilating and incorporating them into his analytic edifice...But he couldn't accept these ideas in the original form...This was a trait of his personality. If people say that Freud was intolerant, in certain ways he was! But we need to understand the meaning of it. I would say that it was a fusion of two opposites: open-mindedness and intolerance.[28]

Weiss told me that Federn had advised him never to approach Freud when he was alone, and immersed in his own thoughts, lest he be irritated. According to Jung's character typology, Weiss thought Freud was a narcissistic obsessional type in which the "thinking function" prevailed. Although Weiss knew enough not to cite Jungian categories to Eissler, Weiss was unknowingly echoing Fritz Wittels's pioneering initial biography of Freud that was written while Freud was still alive and able to comment on it:

> Freud's design in the promotion of these gatherings [in Vienna] was to have his own thoughts passed through the filter of other trained intelligences. It did not matter if the intelligences were mediocre. Indeed, he had little desire that these associates should be persons of strong individuality, that they should be critical and ambitious collaborators. The realm of psychoanalysis was his idea and his will, and he welcomed anyone who accepted his views. What he wanted was to look into a kaleidoscope lined with mirrors that would multiply the images he introduced into it...[H]e

> finds it a nuisance when lights other than his own are thrown athwart his path, or when others try to push him forward or to divert him from his chosen course. Whenever necessary he erects outworks to cut off inconvenient cross-lights...[T]he thoughts of others do not help, but rather hinder, this marvelous man's thought processes. When others try to introduce their thoughts into his system, he denies them hospitality. He can only come back to such thought after a long detour, and by way of cryptomnesia [hidden memory].[29]

For Weiss there were some borrowings in Freud from Adler, for example about Adler's idea about the fusion of aggression and libido, where Freud had not mentioned Adler "*at all.*"

> Freud said only that someone (referring obliquely to Adler) thought he had arrived at this insight previously, but that what he himself was saying was something completely different and new. And this was true, because according to Adler the aggression was primary as a protest in connection with the urge to be on top..., you know, a will to power, whereas Freud arrived at it from the concept of the death drive as a primary instinct which was something *completely* different from the origin of aggression in Adler's opinion. But Freud should have mentioned, I think, how Adler's concept...differed from his own concept. This tendency to ignore and depreciate views divergent from his own was a characteristic of Freud's.[30]

An allied tendency in Freud, Weiss told Eissler, was to form "quite strong counter-transferences...to some patients—and especially to pupils who accepted him." Here Weiss expounded on how Freud had allowed himself to be taken in by Levi-Bianchini, whom Weiss called "a charlatan." Weiss told Eissler, as he did me, that Levi-Bianchini had hindered Weiss's progress in forming a Psychoanalytic Society in Italy because "no intelligent man took him seriously."

> He called himself Professor because in Italy everybody who taught in the University, something equivalent to the German *Dozent*, could call himself Professor. And such *Dozentur* could be achieved in Italy through examinations. Levi-Bianchini took the examinations two or three times until he passed them, and so he was teaching and could call himself "Professor." Nobody took him seriously because he didn't write *one* thing that made sense. He was verbose and un-intelligent, and he didn't understand anything. But he had the idea of introducing Freud to Italy, and before I started translating Freud he asked permission to publish a translation of Freud's little book on *Der Traum* [*On Dreams*] and also the *Three Contributions to Sexuality*...And this was enough to gain Freud's approval. Here was someone who was a professor and who had asked Freud for a translation and

showed recognition of this theory, and Freud was always very much touched and very grateful for anything of this kind. But I understand how much Freud must have suffered from rejection. And that in Germany and Austria everybody must have belittled him and aggressively attacked him. And whenever he saw that somebody *did* recognize him, someone having some official position, he developed a very strong sympathy for this person.

Weiss remained unremitting about Levi-Bianchini:

He *invented* meetings of such a Society, and faked minutes of the meetings. He had a psychiatric hospital near Naples, and he listed the names of all his assistants at the hospital as members of his so-called Society, though none of these assistants had any idea as to what analysis was. He faked it all, nothing was true. And Freud wrote him a letter of gratitude, not realizing that it was all a misrepresentation. Later on, when I discovered that none of these people knew what analysis was, that no meeting had ever taken place except in this man's fantasy, I wrote about it to Freud.

Freud had

replied that he agreed with me, adding that he knew that everyone has good and bad qualities. And, he said, we must not forget that very often the form precedes the content. But I think Freud must have been displeased with the whole thing. Yet he was very much emotionally involved in his sympathy towards adherents of analysis. And he thought that Levi-Bianchini was comparable to a German Privatdozent or something of the kind, not realizing that this title meant much less in Italy than in Germany. It was too late when he realized the true situation.

Weiss went on with Eissler about the problem with Levi-Bianchini:

When I translated Freud's *Introductory Lectures* into Italian, in 1921-22, he asked me to allow Levi-Bianchini to publish them. Freud told me that Levi-Bianchini, who was also an editor, wanted to publish Italian translations of all Freud's books in his collection of psychoanalytical works. And Freud asked me to please let him publish my translation of the Lectures...And so I gave my translation to Levi-Bianchini to publish. I paid all the expenses from my own pocket, 12,000 Lire at the time for a thousand copies of my translation of the *Introductory Lectures*. And Levi-Bianchini did not send me the proofs for correction, but put before me a fait accompli. He commenced with a stupid introduction and he left in 400 typographical errors. All of my pleasure in my translation was spoiled...Very few copies of the book were sold. Later on, it appeared in a new edition, in which Levi-Bianchini played no part, after the second World War.[31]

Weiss could cite further examples of Freud's credulity about possible supporters in Italy. A journalist might write to Freud for permission to publish an article about him, Weiss could advise him not to consent because neither of them could know what kind of people would write the pieces, but then Freud would accept, and then ruefully conclude that he should not have encouraged the articles to come out. As great a controversialist as Freud always remained, he could remain apparently naïve about propagandizing. Although Weiss was always interesting on Freud as a leader, I thought it was in connection with Freud as a clinician that Weiss had a unique contribution to make.

Notes

1. This was also the case in Eissler's interview with Wilhelm Reich, as well as others. See for example *Reich Speaks of Freud*, ed. Mary Higgins and Chester M. Raphael (New York: Noonday Press, 1967), pp. 3-128.
2. Paul Roazen, *The Historiography of Psychoanalysis* (New Brunswick, NJ: Transaction Publishers, 2000), pp. 447-52.
3. Ibid., pp. 106-07.
4. Charles B. Strozier, *Heinz Kohut: The Making of a Psychoanalyst* (New York: Farrar, Straus and Giroux, 2001), pp. 87, 92-93.
5. "Eissler Interview with Weiss, Dec. 13, 1952," (Library of Congress), p. 3.
6. Ibid.
7. Paul Roazen, *Encountering Freud: The Politics and Histories of Psychoanalysis* (New Brunswick, NJ: Transaction Publishers, 1990), ch. 6, "The Tausk Problem," pp. 95-119. Also see Roazen, *On the Freud Watch: Public Memoirs* (London: Free Association Books, 2003), ch. 5, "The Eissler Problem," pp. 58-80.
8. Kurt R. Eissler, *Freud and the Seduction Theory: A Brief Love Affair* (Madison, CT: International Universities Press, 2002), p. 487.
9. Paul Roazen, *Meeting Freud's Family* (Amherst: University of Massachusetts Press, 1993), pp. 130-31.
10. Edoardo Weiss to Bertram Lewin, April 9, 1961, along with two letters from Ernst Federn to Edoardo Weiss, and Bertram Lewin to Edoardo Weiss, April 19, 1961 (Library of Congress). I am once again grateful to Henry Cohen for assisting me in getting copies of these documents.
11. "Eissler Interview," pp. 4-5.
12. Ibid., p. 6.
13. Ibid., p. 9.
14. Ibid.
15. Ibid., p. 11.
16. Ibid.

17. Ibid., pp. 11-12.
18. Ibid., p. 12.
19. Ibid. See Paul Roazen, *Brother Animal: The Story of Freud and Tausk* (New Brunswick, NJ: Transaction Publishers, 1990), chapter 3, pp. 59-93
20. Paul Roazen, *Helene Deutsch: A Psychoanalyst's Life* (New Brunswick, NJ: Transaction Publishers, 1992), p. 173.
21. Paul Roazen, *Encountering Freud: The Politics and Histories of Psychoanalysis* (New Brunswick, NJ: Transaction Publishers), ch. 6. See also Paul Roazen, "Reading, Writing, and Memory: Kurt R. Eissler's Thinking," *Contemporary Psychoanalysis*, Vol. 14, No. 2 (1978), pp. 345-53. See also Roazen, *On the Freud Watch: Public Memoirs* (London: Free Association Books, 2003), ch. 5, "The Eissler Problem."
22. "Eissler Interview," pp. 12-13.
23. "The Interpretation of Dreams," *Standard Edition* (London: Hogarth Press, 1953-74), Vol. 5, pp. 472, 483. See also Paul Roazen, *Freud and His Followers* (New York: Alfred A. Knopf, 1974), p. 32.
24. "Eissler Interview," p. 13.
25. Ibid., pp. 13-14.
26. "On Narcissism," *Standard Edition*, Vol. 14, pp. 92-93; Weiss, *Sigmund Freud as a Consultant*, p. 57.
27. "Eissler Interview," pp. 14-15.
28. Ibid., pp. 33-34.
29. Fritz Wittels, *Sigmund Freud* (New York: Dodd, Mead & Co., 1924), pp. 134, 150, 195.
30. Ibid., pp. 15-16.
31. Ibid., pp. 16-19.

Edoardo Weiss

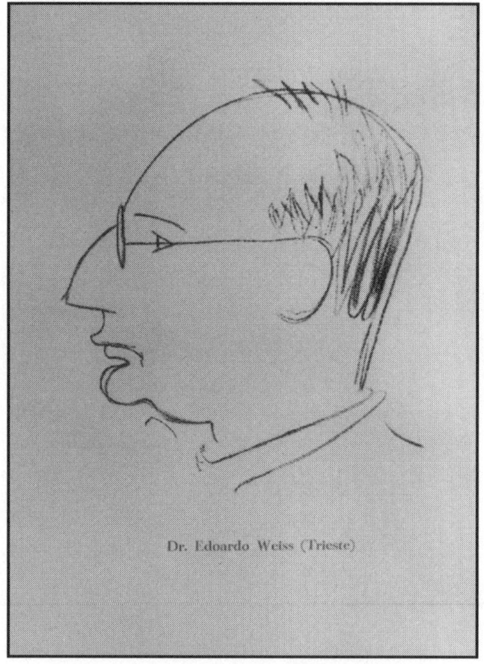

Edoardo Weiss, by Olga Székely-Kovács

Trieste

The Weiss family. Standing (left to right): Paola, Giorgina, Ottocaro, Ida, Gemma, Edoardo. Seated (left to right): Ernesto, Fortuna, Ignazio, Amalia

Italo Svevo with his wife and daughter

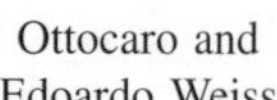

Ottocaro and Edoardo Weiss

Sigmund Freud

Paul Federn

Guido, Edoardo, and Emilio Weiss

Concetta Forzano

Wanda and Edoardo Weiss

IPA Lucerne Congress in 1934

Anna Freud and Edoardo Weiss

Melaine Klein and Edoardo Weiss

Emilio Servedio, Edoardo Weiss, and Nicola Perrotti

7

The Psychoanalytic Family

Even if Eissler cannot have been pleased with what Weiss had had to report about Freud's special kind of "intolerance" as a leader, Weiss's material about Freud's concrete clinical practices had to be of precious and enduring historical interest. Weiss was himself so unusually kind and compassionate a therapist that, in comparison, Freud himself has to sound relatively standoffish about a variety of human foibles. Of course, Weiss was thirty-three years younger than Freud, and therefore that much closer to our own contemporary standards and perspectives. Seeing Freud in historical and social context is one of the hardest challenges facing any of today's students of the history of ideas.

Still, it can be enlightening to follow Weiss's view of Freud's clinical preferences. "First of all," Weiss maintained to Eissler, Freud "was very much against psychopaths." (I think that in talking with Eissler, Weiss was more likely intending to refer to delinquency, rather than formal psychopaths. But according to classical psychiatry, a psychopath is someone lacking in conscience; a more up-to-date way of referring to such people would be the term sociopathic, what once were known as imposters or con artists.) Freud "was not interested in their analysis, and he spoke of them as if they lacked an ego." Weiss thought that "if some patient were too unethical, or disturbed him, Freud completely lost interest in him...he could not stand such people...." Freud also "didn't like perversions, and especially didn't appreciate addictions."[1]

Of course, Freud had in his earliest clinical practice been involved with prematurely recommending the drug cocaine, before its addictive qualities were established.[2] And Freud's own cigar smoking (twenty a day) represented an addiction of his own to nicotine; the narrator in Svevo's *Confessions of Zeno* is prominently concerned with his "last cigarette," perhaps enough in itself to put Freud off the novel. Unknown to Weiss then, Freud did not, in fact, fail to accept dealing with addictive problems in some people, such as Loe Kann or Ruth Mack Brunswick, that he especially admired, but Weiss was generalizing on the basis of the patients he had personally talked about with Freud.[3] It is true that analysts nowadays are unlikely to allow themselves the indulgence of any such moralistic preferences that Freud could participate in, and a broad set of concepts have been added to make a more comprehensive variety of patients seem accessible to therapeutic influence. Without hindsight it is hard to be clear about the extent of implicit political correctness in our own thinking.

Eissler had adopted a quiet interviewing technique with Weiss, rarely interjecting his own views as he tried to encourage the flow of Weiss's associations; as we have seen, at no point did Eissler basically challenge Weiss, or object to his view of things. When Weiss had sent copies of his Freud letters to Jones in London, Weiss had tried to provide the background material on which only Weiss could be expert. Although I adopted no such straightforward letter-by-letter tactic myself, and was far more apt than Eissler to ask Weiss direct questions of my own, still I think there was not one of Freud's letters to Weiss, which subsequently appeared in print, that I did not get to discuss with him.

My interviewing of Weiss was enriched by my having had a chance to read through Eissler's own earlier sessions with him. I had to assume that with Eissler Weiss was eager not to get into more hot water with the powers-that-then-existed, for Weiss told me how he had worried that one of his pieces that appeared in a book edited by Alexander and Helen Ross in 1952 had been editorially changed in such a way as possibly to offend Eissler's rigid sense of orthodoxy. Alexander's outlook might sound unduly manipulative, in contrast to the apparent neutrality of Freud's own therapeutic recommendations; others like Ferenczi had earlier tried to highlight the significance of emotional experiencing, in contrast to searching for the recovery of memories. Right up to her death, Anna Freud was combating in print Alexander's proposals about a "corrective emotional experience."[4]

Anna Freud was herself unhappy when the Freud-Weiss letters came out, and she successfully did what she could to make sure that the International Psychoanalytic Library at the Hogarth Press in London did not accept Weiss's *Sigmund Freud as a Consultant.* (Her intervention on issues of publication matters was not that unusual, and she worked against other analysts than Weiss. She once tried to use her influence with David Astor to fire the analyst Dr. Charles Rycroft as a book reviewer for the London *Observer.*) As she wrote about Weiss's book in 1970 to Masud Khan, then an acknowledged leader[5]:

> To my mind it is a worth less [sic] book in every respect and not even the [Freud] letters can redeem it. Instead [of] increasing the interest in publications of my father's correspondence, it may only do the opposite, i.e. make the public tired and slightly contemptuous of it…I think Grotjahn's Foreword is exaggerated, making the letters look more important than they are. Of course, my father wrote letters like that all the time since many people among the analysts asked him for advice and he was very patient and careful in giving it. His attitude to Edoardo Weiss was in no way different from his attitude to many young colleagues to whom he gave encouragement from a distance. His sympathy was especially with those who had to be pioneers in new areas since he knew from experience how difficult that is...You are right about [Weiss's] own contribution, of course. It is ambivalent, ungrateful and somehow mean; but it is also shallow and on a low level intellectually. There is really no reason why readers have to be exposed to it…My father really showed him nothing but interest and helpfulness…. [T]he translation…is sloppy and inexact.[6]

Anna Freud obviously had no faith in the public's own capacity to sort out the good from the bad; the ideal of toleration presupposes that the truth will emerge from the open marketplace of ideas. In reality, however, no other extant collection of Freud's letters to this day so exclusively focuses on clinical issues. In commenting negatively on this book proposal, Anna Freud was writing to Khan as an intimate advisor. He had at least said to her that the letters

> certainly read very well, and of course they are very exciting material. One has not seen Professor Freud in this particular stance of advising about patients so directly and freely anywhere else, and in this sense they are a valuable addition to the Freud literature. Dr. Weiss does a very good job of providing the relevant material about the cases, which help one understand the letters.[7]

Even Anna Freud had commented to Khan about these letters: "They cannot help being interesting, in spite of everything, at least to us."

But an unspoken aspect of Anna Freud's reluctance to help the book forward in England was that it contained for the first time in print, in a 1935 letter of her father's, confirmation of Freud's own analysis of her. Khan had raised this precise point, although he told her that he had to "confess" to her that he found it "embarrassing to broach [it] with you." Concerning the one 1935 letter about her analysis by her father, Khan thought

> This, of course, will immediately attract everybody's attention. Weiss himself makes no comment on the letter, which only leaves it for gossip-mongers to put their own constructions. I do not know what could have been done by way of annotation here, but somehow I feel that a judicious statement about the issue by way of explication could help.
>
> I do want to reiterate that, in my judgment, the letters of Professor Freud are of great value to the tradition of psychoanalysis, and particularly in terms of his opinion about the analyzability of cases and other clinical matters.

Khan was writing not only as editor of the International Psychoanalytic Library, but also as one of the directors of the Freud Copyrights. But Anna Freud chose not to comment in any way to Khan on the existence of that key 1935 letter. And Anna Freud's official biographer chose to omit the matter of Anna Freud's silence to Khan from the selective quotation she published of Anna Freud's about the Freud-Weiss correspondence.[8]

The very first letters from Freud to Weiss are important not just because we have a chance to listen to Freud discuss a patient he and Weiss had in common, but for the reason that they help to account for some of Freud's views on the tangled issue of the translations of his works. For in authorizing Weiss in 1919 to translate the *Introductory Lectures on Psychoanalysis*, Freud specifically said: "I also give you the right to make such changes as you consider necessary and I am convinced that you will make the right selection."[9]

Much recent controversy in the English-speaking world has existed about the way Freud's works were rendered into English by James Strachey, someone whose translations Freud was delighted with, and following Freud's death Anna Freud had assisted Strachey in an almost incredibly detailed way. Nonetheless Bruno Bettelheim in particular blamed the Strachey version for having unnecessarily made Freud's work sound falsely scientific; Bettelheim also criticized those works edited by Strachey for having militated against the practice of lay analysis.[10] Yet none of the main translators, Strachey as well as Anna Freud, were themselves medically trained, and I have felt that Freud was lucky in getting someone as unusually literate in English as Strachey to take charge single-handedly of the English edition of Freud's writings.[11]

The example of Weiss in Italy shows how free a hand Freud extended to his disciples; he was not thinking in terms of their producing sacred texts but was concerned rather that his basic ideas be as widely disseminated as possible. As Freud reiterated to Weiss in 1920, "the way in which you translate dreams, slips, and mistakes, by substituting the examples of your own, is of course the only right procedure. To my regret I have no assurance that this will be done correctly in the other translations which mostly are not made by analysts."[12] Although Freud's letters to his early translator in America, A. A. Brill, have not yet been published, my suspicion is that Freud gave him, in person or by letter, similar license as well. (Freud's own translations as a young man could be as controversial as everything else in his career.[13]) Yet Brill has been regularly criticized for doing exactly what Freud authorized Weiss to undertake—substituting his own examples for those of Freud. Strachey himself stuck much more closely to the literal texts.

Two of Weiss's sisters who were in analysis with Freud come up in this correspondence. One of them, whom Weiss sent to Freud for treatment in January 1921 when she was thirty-five years old, Weiss described in print as "Mrs. L. M.," disguised as supposedly "a friend of my family." (Weiss confided to me that he thought that his brother Ottocaro would be offended if he disclosed her true identity.) Weiss wrote: "Since she was a friend of my family I could not take her in treatment. I had sent her first to a friend of mine, a psychologist, who treated her under my supervision. Then I realized that she needed a more experienced analyst."[14] Freud wrote back to Weiss about her:

> I am very fond of her. For the time being it goes very well. Her seriousness and her intelligence are very welcome helpers. Naturally some difficulties are waiting for us somewhere, but they shall not frighten us. The prepara-

> tory treatment with your friend certainly did no harm, at least I have the benefit of it, for she arrived with much understanding. This treatment could not succeed 1) because your friend is a young man and she felt too much embarrassed, 2) because he had to stand up against the entire first onslaught of resistance, 3) because she needed a person fit for a father transference. Perhaps he also had opened up too much in too short a time.[15]

Her first name was Amalia, the same as Freud's mother, and Weiss agreed with me that this must have played a significant role in Freud's special liking for this sister. Freud wrote a lot about the magic of names. Amalia was helped by Freud for about half a year; he had then dismissed her from treatment, promising that he would take her back if she should need it.

Weiss was on good enough terms with this older sister of his that he heard from her many aspects of Freud's analytic approach. Once with Freud she was in a bad mood, saying, "life should not exist," and asking why she should continue to live. Freud answered: "I can understand why someone says that; it is a legitimate position. But since I am a physician, I have chosen to stand for the preservation of life." Weiss was impressed that Freud had not said that her arguments or point of view were basically wrong; and he took it to be an example of Freud's pessimism.

Weiss also found confirmation from this sister that Freud could have a sense of humor about his clinical practices. Weiss quoted her as having said to him that Freud had once remarked in the analysis: "If the Psychoanalytic Society knew what I was doing I would be kicked out." Among Freud's continental disciples, though, it was widely known how unorthodox in technique he could be; at his best Freud viewed each of his patients as an exception.

Americans in particular seemed naïve about the technologies of psychoanalytic technique, whether it concerned the use of the couch or the relative silence of the analyst. Freud wrote his recommendations on technique in a series of pre-World War I papers, at the time he was having disagreements with people like Adler and Jung; Freud seemed determined to differentiate his way of doing things from that of those he deemed errant, backsliding disciples, as he sought to establish a separate discipline of his own. But even then, Freud was cautiously specifying that these were recommendations suitable for beginners to keep in mind, examples of how he had himself once been inclined to go wrong. But in Jung's case, for instance, there is no indication when Freud and he were on the best of terms that Jung was likely to use a couch in the course of his treatments, nor any sign then that Freud objected. The Berlin school of analysts, one that only got going in the 1920s, was far more likely to formalize rules than Freud himself.

At one point in Freud's analysis of Weiss's sister Amalia she had been embarrassed about something, and did not want him to look at her. Freud then proceeded to get up from his chair behind her, and walked in front of the couch to face her directly. He told her then that she had to have the courage to face him. So in practice Freud was not inclined to be a stick-in-the-mud about the use of the couch, although as we shall see he could chastise Weiss for being too indulgent to one of his patients in allowing her to sit up.

After the interruption Amalia was eager to return to analysis with Freud, and Weiss interceded in her behalf. "When Freud dismissed Mrs. L. M., he had promised to take her back for more treatment if she should need it. However, when she asked him to take her back, he answered her that at that time he was too busy. If she was in great need of relief, he advised her to return to my friend the psychologist who had started her analysis."[16] Freud wrote Weiss in 1922: "I hope that Mrs. L. M. is already well adjusted or that she has turned to your friend, since I am over-burdened."[17] In those days Freud was increasingly concentrating on training pupils from abroad. Since Amalia "begged" Weiss "to write to Freud, to remind him that he had promised to take her back into treatment if she should need it," Freud answered Weiss accordingly on April 3, 1922.

> I answer you and ask you to give this information to Mrs. L. M.
>
> I know what I promised her and was certainly prepared to keep my promise. I was, however, not prepared for the extent to which I would be kept busy with a stream of students from abroad. Out of nine people, I now have only one patient—and since some of them have remained longer than they intended I am now under such pressure that A. F. Meijer, for example, the well-known Dutch analyst, has been waiting in vain since September to be called for his analysis.
>
> It would, therefore, have been a great relief if I had heard that Mrs. L. M. had been able to complete her treatment with your friend. Since this is not the case, I will abide by my promise, that I will see her as soon as I have a free hour. I can neither increase my workload nor go back on commitments made three-quarters of a year ago. If the near future—I close on the first of July—does not bring unexpected free time, then I will find her in my waiting room on the 30th of September.[18]

(In writing his commentary on the Freud letters for Jones, Weiss volunteered that this letter had been written about Weiss's "older sister."[19])

Freud was clearly giving preference to Amalia because she was Weiss's sister. So in spite of his busy schedule with analytic students in training from abroad Freud did in fact again take her in analysis. She was once more with him in the spring of 1922; altogether she had a little over a year of Freud's treatment. In April 1922 Freud told Amalia that a young man in the waiting room had been the boy in Freud's famous case history of "Little Hans."[20] Weiss thought he had told her that because she was Weiss's sister, and therefore should share in the early history of his discipline. Freud frequently used the story of early psychoanalysis as part of building his following.

On January 7, 1923 Freud once more wrote about Amalia to Weiss: she

> has again learned much this time and I hope with lasting benefit. Unpleasant reality stands in the way of a thorough dissolution of the neurosis. Therefore I am not quite reassured about her future. New education and taming of her gruesome sadism and of her excessive behavior seems really possible, but it would require continuous influence over a long time.[21]

Weiss said that although Freud had been "very good" for her, he had "not quite finished" analyzing Amalia; in the treatment of her obsessions her "aggressions" had come out. (According to Freud's theory of how psychological opposite go together, sadism underlies a compulsive façade.) When she had thoughts about suicide, Freud had told her that he was not worried about this obsessiveness: "You are so ambivalent, sometimes saying yes and then again no, that you cannot make a decision. There is no danger." As it turned out, European history dealt savagely with Amalia; she and her husband made the bad decision to remain in Trieste during World War II, and wound up among those gassed to death by the Nazis at Auschwitz.

Freud charged Weiss for the consultations he had with him; in one of the letters about "Mrs. L. M." Freud instructed Weiss that the fee should be sent to Freud's sister-in-law Minna, who was then on holiday and doubtless appreciated the extra money. In contrast to how Anna Freud later tried to describe Weiss as just a run-of-the-mill younger colleague of her father's, Freud had concluded that January 7, 1923 letter about Amalia by complimenting Weiss unstintingly: "I think with satisfaction of your unshakeable conviction, your willingness to sacrifice and your restless industriousness, and I wish you fulfilling success in the new year."[22]

Over time I became personally acquainted with enough of Freud's continental pupils to have experienced the full import of the old Viennese charm, which could attract and yet hold at a distance at the same time. Another side of that special tact and kindliness, however, can be considered *politesse* or *schmaltz*. As a naïve American I still interpret the conclusion of Freud's Jan. 7, 1923 letter to Weiss as having intended high praise. But Anna Freud might have also been correct in skeptically seeing through the habitual insincerities of her father as a cultivated gentleman of that era. One of Anna Freud's own American patients, Esther Menaker, once commented that she "always experienced as hypocrisy" in the Viennese their "elaborate, ritualized, exaggerated politeness...."[23]

But it counts in favor of Freud's unusually good opinion of Weiss that he also saw Georgina, a younger sister of Weiss's, in analysis. Unfortunately Freud "did not have good contact with her" and did not succeed in helping her "much." Freud later sent Georgina, whom he had thought a hysteric, for further analysis in Vienna with Helene Deutsch after he had been unsuccessful with her. This sister even went with Helene Deutsch when she herself undertook an analysis (1923-24) in Berlin with Karl Abraham; it was typical then for patients to tag along with their analysts, for example on holidays, rather than to interrupt analysis. According to what Helene Deutsch subsequently thought, Georgina was so hysterical that the diagnosis of a "neurosis" as opposed to schizophrenia was never a settled matter; she was a little paranoid and, despite conversion symptoms, not easy to get in contact with.[24] Later on, despite a good therapeutic result with Helene Deutsch, Georgina became manifestly schizophrenic, and spent at least twenty years living in an Australian mental hospital; she had the delusion that the Nazis were influencing her after they had supposedly taken away her brain. Presumably she moved in response to her hallucinations, and therefore could not take care of herself.

Weiss used her disguised case history in a mid-1960s article of his. He was trying to illustrate Federn's concept of a weak ego in schizophrenia, as opposed to Freud's own classical psychoanalytic view that schizophrenics have an excess of narcissism. Federn's point of view was designed to encourage therapists to lend assistance to such patients, rather than be clinically repudiating of them.

> In Federn's concept a weak ego, and I am thinking particularly of the schizophrenic ego, is poorly supplied with cathexis. Therefore, it is less able than a normal ego to extend itself either over actual objects or over their autoplastically built substitutes. In schizophrenia the ego withdraws from external objects not because it has an excess of ego libido, or narcissism, at the expense of object libido, but, on the contrary, because of economic necessity....

Psychoanalysts mean by "economic" questions ones having to do with a quantity of mental forces; "cathexis" referred to the investment of energy:

> A schizophrenic ego is not sufficiently supplied with ego cathexis for its own functions. And, in an attempt to spare ego cathexis, in order to slow down the process of its own disintegration, it must give up both object love and identifications. This is very apparent in the disintegration of the superego in schizophrenic patients. Although the ego cathexis adheres in general more tenaciously to internalized objects than to external objects, melancholic patients stick more firmly to all internalized objects than do schizophrenic patients. A patient may cease loving his parents and at the same time he may maintain his identification with them.

I wish to illustrate briefly such a paranoid schizophrenic state by one example. Weiss proceeded to change the gender of his sister Georgina, as well as several of the particular details of her family history:

> The patient is a 42-year old male refugee from Germany. He comes from a family of 10 children. He is the third youngest of the children, evidently an unwanted child. His relation to his neurotic mother has been very poor. She had to devote much time and attention to some of his siblings who needed her care very badly, because they were in poor physical condition. So, the patient must have been very much neglected by his mother in his childhood. Later, some of his siblings ridiculed him for his endeavors to gain general admiration for his intellectual achievements. When he grew up he showed a poor capacity for relating himself to other people and manifested other neurotic symptoms also. The task of integrating the identifications with the persons of his Jewish environment with those of the Nazi popula-

> tion was much too great for his ego. And when he came to this country his ego had, in addition, to adjust itself to the American environment. In this situation his ego broke down.

Weiss went on to describe what he told me was her "mono-symptom" requiring hospitalization, even though she could have a tender relation with her grandchildren.

> He has acoustic hallucinations and suffers from the delusion of being influenced by criminals in Germany. They use all kinds of waves, telepathy and other devices to destroy his intelligence and his personality. They even force upon him the dreams which they want him to have. And they do all this to him because they envy him for his intelligence, and also because they obtain sadistic gratification from such persecutions. For a long time this patient refused to speak or write in German to his friends and to his family, because he feared that his German enemies might intercept his thoughts. They did not understand English. His last description of his delusional state was the following:
>
> "I am the victim of a horrible crime which is perpetrated by hundreds of minds. Mental forces are injected into my brain day and night. While I am sleeping they enter through my mouth. They take possession of my brain and have almost torn it out from my head. They treat my brain as if it belonged to them. It is useless to talk about this to my doctors in the hospital because they think that I have delusions. In order not to appear insane to them I decided to keep my mouth shut from now on. Please help me. These criminals have left me only as much of my brain as I need to survive physically." From this letter, written to a friend of his, we can clearly understand how much his ego cathexis is impaired.[25]

Weiss was evidently quoting from a letter Georgina had sent to him in Chicago. When I read this case fragment to Helene Deutsch about her former patient, she was quietly amused ("such things!") at how Weiss had altered his sister's gender and the geography. Weiss had been hoping that through his contact with me Helene Deutsch might now want to write to Georgina, but she declined; he himself thought it might be useless for her to contact Georgina. Since Weiss had been so well-informed about Freud's counter-transferences to his patients, I asked Weiss: *Which of the two sisters had Freud preferred*? Without hesitation he thought Freud had liked best the older one, since she was an obsessional type, intelligent, honest, and serious.

Notes

1. "Eissler Interview," op. cit., pp. 23, 24, 28.
2. Roazen, *Freud and His Followers* (New York: Alfred A. Knopf, 1974), pp. 67-70. Roazen, *How Freud Worked: First-Hand Accounts of Patients* (Northvale, NJ: Jason Aronson, 1995), pp. 4-9.
3. Roazen, *Freud and His Followers*, pp. 355-56, 427-37.
4. Joseph Sandler, Hansi Kennedy, Robert L. Tyson, *The Technique of Child Psychoanalysis: Discussions with Anna Freud* (Cambridge, MA: Harvard University Press, 1980), pp. 70, 96, 110-11, 113.
5. Paul Roazen, *The Historiography of Psychoanalysis* (New Brunswick, NJ: Transaction Publishers, 2000), pp. 297-300; Roazen, *The Trauma of Freud: Controversies in Psychoanalysis* (New Brunswick, NJ: Transaction Publishers, 2002), pp. 246-51.
6. Anna Freud to Masud Khan, July 12, 1970 (Library of Congress). I am indebted to Henry Cohen for sending me copies of the relevant Anna Freud-Khan correspondence.
7. Masud Khan to Anna Freud, July 7, 1970 (Library of Congress).
8. See Elisabeth Young-Bruehl, *Anna Freud: A Biography* (New York: Summit Books, 1988), p. 434. Also Roazen, *The Trauma of Freud*, pp 93-110.
9. Edoardo Weiss, *Sigmund Freud as a Consultant: Recollections of a Pioneer in Psychoanalysis*, with an introduction by Martin Grotjahn (New York: Intercontinental Medical Book Corporation, 1970; New Brunswick, NJ: Transaction Publishers, 1991), p. 24.
10. Bruno Bettelheim, *Freud and Man's Soul* (New York: Alfred A. Knopf, 1982).
11. Roazen, *The Historiography of Psychoanalysis*, op. cit., pp. 105, 116, 145, 345, 348-49, 409-10, 412-13, 430.
12. Weiss, *Sigmund Freud as a Consultant*, p. 29.
13. Ernest Jones, *Sigmund Freud: Life and Work*, Vol. 1, *The Young Freud 1856-1900*, 2nd edition (London: The Hogarth Press, 1956), p. 251. See also Michael Molnar, "John Stuart Mill Translated by Siegmund Freud," *Psychoanalysis and History*, Vol. 1 (2), 1999, pp. 195-205.
14. Weiss, *Sigmund Freud as a Consultant*, p. 30.
15. Ibid., pp. 30-31.
16. Ibid., p. 32.
17. Ibid., p. 33.
18. Ibid., pp. 33-34.
19. Edoardo Weiss to Ernest Jones, June 30, 1956, "Commentary."
20. See the "Postcript" to the Little Hans case history that Freud wrote in 1922: *Standard Edition*, Vol. 10 (London: Hogarth Press, 1953-74), pp. 148-49.
21. Weiss, *Sigmund Freud as a Consultant*, p. 39.
22. Ibid.

23. Esther Menaker, *Appointment in Vienna* (New York: St. Martin's Press, 1989), p.13. This book has been reprinted as *Misplaced Loyalties* (New Brunswick, NJ: Transaction Publishers, 1995), with a new introduction by Paul Roazen.
24. Interview with Helene Deutsch, no. 41, July 2, 1966. (Paul Roazen Collection, Boston University).
25. Edoardo Weiss, "Vicissitudes of Internalized Objects in Paranoid Schizophrenia and Manic-depressive States," *Psychoanalytic Review*, Vol. 50 (Winter 1963-64), pp. 599-600

8

Clinical Moralism

Throughout Freud's letters to Weiss about patients, a moralistic tone appears, even though it may seem out of keeping with what one now thinks of in connection with an analyst's so-called neutrality. Historical distance is necessary: our own era's forms of moralism can take the form of various illusions of superiority, that we are the best, and the past misguided. Like the rest of us, Freud had his decided human preferences, and the particular moralism that shows up in the letters to Weiss was a typical aspect of Freud's own characteristic clinical approach as a whole. Freud could, for example, describe some patients he admired as "worthy" of psychoanalysis. It has to remain a bit startling to find Freud, in a famous 1912 paper, referring in passing to "a person even of only moderate worth,"[1] since so much of Christian culture has paid at least lip service to the preciousness and significance of every single human soul. The concept of worthiness logically implies the possibility that some people could be deemed worthless.[2]

In the context of all the authoritarian clinical practices of his own day, Freud can fairly be considered unusually tolerant. It was, after all, an era when mental illness was commonly blamed on the supposed evil practice of masturbation, or the consequences of reputed "degeneracy." But in hindsight, it is striking how he could be surprisingly explicit in his judgment-making: "A good, capable, conscientious woman will speak no better of herself after she develops melancholia than one who is in fact worthless; indeed, the former is perhaps more likely to fall ill of the disease than the latter, of whom we too should have nothing good to say."[3]

To take one important example of Freud's moralistic outlook, Freud had had in treatment with him in 1911 a patient whom Weiss in print called "Dr. A.," who later went to others for analysis, and finally ended up back in analysis with Weiss in Trieste after World War I. (He also had seen in Vienna first the analyst Isidor Sadger, before Freud, and afterwards Victor Tausk, Rudolf Reitler, as well as Abraham in Berlin in 1914. Freud wrote Abraham that he was "a bad case…an enigma, probably a *mavais sujet*, up to now nothing could be done with him."[4]) Now this "Dr. A." suffered, according to Weiss, "from some addictions and lived a very disturbed life."[5] It turns out that this "Dr. A." was a classmate of Weiss's in Trieste, the younger brother of Svevo's wife, Livia Veneziani Svevo: Dr. Bruno Veneziani (1890-1952).[6] She described him as "her father's favorite, the only boy," who studied chemistry and music.[7] Weiss's younger son Guido, a distinguished mathematician, considered him a "cultured" person.

Dr. Veneziani was also homosexual, and had expressed anti-Semitic thoughts to Freud, which Freud had "resented and showed it" in the analysis. (Tausk had not been "so negative" about Dr. Veneziani as Freud.) In 1919, Weiss had written to Freud proposing that Dr. Veneziani help Weiss translate into Italian Freud's *Introductory Lectures on Psychoanalysis*: as Weiss described it,

> I asked Dr. A., whom I had sent to Freud in treatment in 1911, whether he would be willing to help me in this delicate work. He was a very intelligent man of my age, well acquainted with psychoanalysis, and with an excellent knowledge of German and Italian. In the beginning, however, I was not aware of his severely neurotic condition and his character traits.

Weiss "soon realized that Dr. A. was too disturbed to be of any help in this work...With his permission I complied with his wish and wrote to Freud asking if he would be willing to take him back into treatment. I wrote several pages describing Dr. A.'s psychological condition."[8]

One of Svevo's best biographers has described his brother-in-law Bruno as someone who in 1910 was "studying to be a concert pianist," but "was sent to Vienna to be analyzed by Freud himself. The treatment did him no good, and he returned two years later, more neurotic than ever, reporting that Freud had pronounced him incurable."[9] Svevo himself left an account of "a neurotic friend of mine" who

> went to Vienna to undergo treatment; the only good that came out of it was the warning it gave to me. He had himself psychoanalyzed and returned from the cure destroyed, as lacking in will-power as before, but with his feebleness aggravated by the conviction that, being as he was, he could not behave otherwise. It was he who convinced me how dangerous it was to explain to a man how he is made, and every time I see him I love him for the sake of our old friendship, but also with this new gratitude.[10]

In a letter, Svevo expressed what one fine literary critic has called a "preference for illness and literature (even if it leads to failure) over cure"; as Svevo put it tersely, "He is a great man, that Freud of ours; but more for novelists than for patients."

> Elsewhere Svevo admits that he developed a distaste, not for Freud the man or thinker but for the idea of psychoanalysis as therapy. Psychoanalysis as a heuristic inquiry was bound to intrigue him. Throughout his work, there are traces of an original trauma, as well as an interest in the expressive structures of dreams and strategies of transfer and repetition. What Svevo dislikes about psychoanalysis is not its theoretical thrust but its claims of clinical cures. Svevo is much too committed to protecting his illness. The ironic link between disease and health, as well as the problematic relation between lies and truths, is at the heart of Svevo's work.[11]

Perhaps it may now be more understandable why Weiss in 1923 responded to Svevo's *The Confessions of Zeno* with a "snub" that was "a natural and fair one from a serious Freudian...Svevo was probably quite ignorant of many sides of Freudian theory, and caricatured some of those he did know."[12] The fact that one of Svevo's nieces, at the age of fifteen, seems to have successfully been treated by Freud in 1911 was evidently not been enough to counterbalance for Svevo what had happened with his brother-in-law Bruno.[13]

Now Freud did reply at some length on October 3, 1920 about Weiss's suggestion that his proposed translating colleague, Bruno Veneziani, return to Freud for further analysis:

> I was indeed surprised when you announced Dr. A. as your co-worker for the translation considering all I knew about him.
>
> Since you are asking me today for a professional report on him, I shall not hesitate to give you my opinion. I believe it is a bad case, one particularly not suitable for free analysis. Two things are missing in him: first, a certain conflict of suffering between his ego and what his drives demand, for he is essentially very well satisfied with himself and suffers only from the antagonism of external conditions. Second, he is lacking a halfway

> normal character of the ego which could cooperate with the analyst. On the contrary he will always strive to mislead the analyst, to trick him and push him aside. Both defects amount actually to one and the same, namely, the development of a fantastically narcissistic, self-satisfied ego which is inaccessible to any influence, and which unfortunately can always claim his talents and personal gifts.
>
> It is also my opinion that nothing would be gained by having him come into treatment with me or anybody else. His future may be to perish in his excesses. It is also possible that he, like Mirabeau, of whose type he may be, may pull himself together and, while continuing all his vices, accomplish some outstanding achievement. But this is not very likely.

Freud was alluding here to a moderate in the French Revolution, Honoré Gabriel Riquetti Mirabeau (1749-1791). A remarkable orator but unusual for his debts and rakishness, he died in bed "of an inflammation of the bowels, caused by excesses."[14] A biography of Mirabeau had appeared in Paris in 1920. In 1928, Freud had used his knowledge of history in writing sympathetically to the mother of an American whom Freud diagnosed as a paranoid schizophrenic: "Even Rousseau was such a case, not less abnormal."[15] Freud had gone on to Weiss, about Dr. Veneziani, claiming, "I do not even consider the fact that he is a homosexual. He could remain that and still live normally and rationally." Weiss felt skeptically about the real bases for Freud's disapproval of Dr. Veneziani.

In writing about Dr. Veneziani to Weiss, Freud seemed to feel that Dr. Veneziani's mother's struggle lent some sympathy to the case, and to that extent Freud saw the patient as a neurotic subject to psychoanalytic influence:

> I also understand that his mother will not give him up without further efforts. The mechanism is after all a neurotic one even in this case, but the dynamics are unfavorable for a change. I therefore recommend that he be sent to an overwhelming, therapeutically effective person in an institution. I know such a man in the person of Dr. Groddeck in Baden-Baden (Sanitarium). Of course he should be informed about the peculiarity of the patient. If he does not want to take him, then Marcinowski in Heilbrun near Tölz (Bavaria) comes under consideration, but he probably will reject him outright.

Freud wound up devastatingly:

> In the most unfavorable cases one ships such people, as Dr. A., across the ocean, with some money, let's say to South America, and lets them there seek and find their destiny.

> If Mrs. A. intends to pay for this expert opinion, let her send 100 lire to Miss Minna Bernays in Meran….(my sister-in-law).[16]

Dr. Veneziani got sent by Weiss to Groddeck for a few months, but "without any therapeutic success." (Although Groddeck has attained some historical stature,[17] Jaroslaw Marcinowski is known only for having been a member of the Vienna Psychoanalytic Society from 1919 until 1925.) Groddeck, someone Weiss thought Freud liked too much because of Groddeck's personal admiration, mishandled the case; at Baden-Baden Dr. Veneziani acquired a new "boyfriend," and Groddeck had approved. Weiss thought that Freud did not truly understand Groddeck's clinical practices. In 1923 Groddeck wrote to Freud of Veneziani's treatment that he had been "proud of it in those days, though it became apparent later on that it was a mistake."[18] Although Freud thought that Dr. Veneziani was "really no good," when he "returned to Italy" Weiss "kept him in supportive therapy. He died several years after my emigration to the States."[19]

Although in Freud's writings he had argued that all psychoanalytic treatment requires the sacrifice of financial expense, in practice Freud could behave otherwise and he treated many people free of charge. (Sometimes such treatment could be because of prior services performed by someone in the family for Freud's cause.[20]) Freud certainly took a dim view of Dr. Veneziani. According to Freud's theories, a "perversion" would mean that there is no neurosis; he viewed them as conceptual opposites, and without a neurosis there was nothing that could be analyzed. Supposedly the problem with perversion was that it discharged libido; that gratification means that there is insufficient self-discontent for the analyst to get a handle to work with.

Freud thought that since Dr. Veneziani's conflicts were not internalized but between the instincts and society he was not analyzable. Weiss did not take seriously Freud's disclaimer about the insignificance to him of Dr. Veneziani's homosexuality. As we saw with "Frank," Freud did not seem in general to rate sexuality very highly, and I suspect that sometimes for him sex was for the Gentile world, and Jews should be more or less above it. Now Freud did write a famous and comforting 1935 letter to an American mother of a male homosexual, and he tolerantly treated someone like James

Strachey.[21] (It also appeared that, in a different context, Weiss was surprised to hear from me how Freud could be clinically approving of a psychoanalytic case of Helene Deutsch's that developed into one of female homosexuality.[22] We now know much more about Freud's capacity to deal with the poet H.D.'s bisexuality.[23]) Unlike Weiss and Tausk, Abraham too had deemed Dr. Veneziani analytically unsuitable: "there is," Abraham wrote Freud, "no getting at his narcissism."[24]

When Freud mentioned the possibility of shipping Dr. Veneziani abroad, Weiss told Eissler that Freud had had in mind an unhappy "destiny"; Freud had "meant either in jail, in suicide, or so forth. This was his attitude toward such patients."[25] Weiss also wrote about this same former patient of Freud's to Jones; Dr. Veneziani was

> a schoolmate of mine from my tenth year on, and since he had been in analysis with Prof. Freud for a few months and later with several other analysts, I contemplated undergoing the translation of Freud's works with his cooperation. Up to that time I knew only of his intelligence, which was very superior, and of his scientific education, but soon thereafter I realized that he was extremely narcissistic, a homosexual, a drug addict, and unable to engage in serious work. In fact, I soon dropped him [as co-translator] and he became my patient.

Weiss told Jones that he thought that thanks to Freud's October 3, 1920 letter about Dr. Veneziani "I was completely informed with regard to the unfavorable dynamics of his ego...Dr. Veneziani died in December, 1952 with a heart attack as a consequences of his long lasting addictions."[26] (Apparently Weiss had eventually sent Dr. Veneziani to Bernhard in Rome.)

Weiss explained to me that by shipping such a person as "Dr. A." abroad Freud meant that he be sent away "so that he might perish." As much as he found the patient distasteful, Freud had so enduringly low an opinion of America that he did not recommend that even Dr. Veneziani be sent there. Later I would be reminded of this case in talking to Anna Freud; for she told me how the "two Americas" were split over Melanie Klein's teachings. Many of Klein's trainees went to South America, where her influence by the mid-1960s had become high. But the idea that there were "two Americas" for Anna Freud was one way, I thought, of her putting the United States in its place.

Weiss also consulted with Freud about patients Freud had never seen, but only heard about by means of Weiss's letters. The first, "a highly educated man in his early forties," ten years Weiss's senior, had earlier always been sexually potent with a deeply loved wife; but she suffered from a deep depression, went to Vienna for an analysis, and committed suicide. This patient told Weiss that "he would have done anything for her recovery; he would even have permitted her to have an extra-marital affair if this had been necessary."[27] Weiss said he thought this was the grounds for Freud's thinking the patient, currently suffering from potency problems, was "obviously a valuable person who deserves to be treated further and may also have a good chance." But Freud had cautioned Weiss:

> It seems that he has not yet opened up to you completely and as long as this is not the case one does not get the material for a reliable judgment. However, six months is not a long time and there is still hope. Perhaps you show him too much impatience and therapeutic ambition, instead of concentrating exclusively on his personal conquest.

When I specifically questioned Weiss about what Freud might have meant by the "personal conquest" of the patient, he replied that Freud was proposing that he enhance the transference "by showing a personal interest" in the patient, showing that Weiss "appreciated his personality."

Freud could have an enormously subtle understanding about unconscious clinical material, and continued about this case:

> Therefore, I think: no setting of a termination date. The difficulty lies obviously in his relationship to a man (the father, with whom he cannot identify you easily.) With regard to masturbation point out to him that through it he would definitely block his normal access to women and that abstinence in spite of occasional lapses would be worthwhile analytically. It is not easy to guess about the other motives which sustain his impotence. Perhaps even his wife was a father substitute for him, and satisfied his feminine traits through her masculine traits.
>
> It cannot be doubted that the motive for his fixed renunciation of women is regret and atonement, thus consciousness of guilt. I do not favor prostitution as a substitute. It is better to let him remain totally abstinent until his abstinence is from time to time interrupted by masturbation. He will not permanently endanger his potency thereby. This is proven by his attitude in his marriage. No attempt to burden him with our more liberal opinions about sexual intercourse. I am not sure that I have anything to offer you with these remarks. The problem is essentially a technical one.

Weiss found that this "patient opened up…more and more as I patiently followed Freud's suggestions." The patient had found in his wife "some of the satisfaction which he had enjoyed in his rapport with his father whom he had lost in his early teens." He gave up seeing prostitutes, controlled masturbation, and after another year and a half of analysis "met a young woman, a teacher, with whom he could have a satisfactory sexual relationship."[28]

In contrast to this case of transient impotency, another one was a Slovene:

> a young man who had been discharged from the army after the first World War. He was sexually impotent. He had betrayed many people and had a very immoral ego. One day I learned that he had told his father that my fee was higher than it actually was. His father paid me in cash, handed to me by the patient, and the patient had been keeping the extra money for himself.

Although Weiss had been reminded of Freud's opinion of Dr. Veneziani, he was hopeful that the patient's ego disturbance might be accessible to "special treatment," like Federn and Aichhorn might have recommended. But Freud's judgment about the Slovene was harsh and outspoken: he was "obviously a scoundrel who is not worth your trouble. Our analytic art is powerless with these people, nor can our insight penetrate the dominant dynamic conditions of such cases. I do not answer him directly. I assume you will send him away." Weiss accordingly "dismissed" from analytic treatment this second case of impotency.[29] As early as 1907 Freud was contrasting "scoundrels" with "neurotics," as he wrote Abraham: "the proof of the pair of opposites seems to me to be the latest result of analysis to date."[30]

Weiss also had in analytic treatment a young depressed painter; Weiss showed some of his paintings to Freud in Vienna. "The patient was the only son of a widow; he had lost his father in childhood," and Weiss "sent Freud a long description of the clinical picture." Freud replied:

> From the theoretically excellent description of your patient I can only understand that he can be considered a "simple depression." This affliction is little studied; it should, however, be accessible to analysis. Keep trying patiently. I should say, as a surmise, that it is a matter of a simple fixation of a high degree on the mother, whom he rejects from time to time,

> so that nothing then is left to him. The difficulty of your position lies certainly in the fact that he has to keep this relation hidden from you as a man, a father substitute. Technically, this is done by his intentionally holding back some idea, so that the analysis then comes to a standstill. Do not let yourself be dissuaded by any disavowal on his part. It happens more often than we suspect. It will interest me to learn whether you can make anything out of these hints.

Freud was cautious and modest in the consulting aid he offered Weiss, who helped the patient become "conscious of his fixation to his mother." His paintings became more "cheerful," although Weiss

> could not find that he was holding back some ideas as Freud had suggested. It became increasingly evident that he had missed his father whom he had lost in early childhood...I made clear to him how the repression of his attachment to his mother, to whom he remained fixed, made his life unhappy. When someone puts all his money in a bank and then forgets where he has put it, he has no spending money.[31]

It sounds like Freud's supervision of Weiss, as well as with that Helene Deutsch, could be genuinely self-denying and agnostic, as when Freud began writing to Weiss about those two earlier cases of impotency: "Because you know so much yourself I cannot easily find where you might have overlooked something."[32]

Freud could be notably encouraging and supportive to Weiss's clinical efforts. In response to a long letter from Weiss about a patient who was threatening to break off an analysis, Freud wrote: "I believe that your patient should not give in to the repetition compulsion, but continue the treatment." Weiss had outlined how the current behavior fit into previous patterns, and Freud offered some complicated interpretations of his own, concluding with an embattled cry against neurotic repetitiveness: "Don't leave him to the demon!" Weiss felt he had learned that it was "not enough" to interpret transference feelings to the patient, and Federn seemed right to warn against interpreting transference with psychotics:

> In the treatment of neurotic patients it is not enough to make the patient remember those feelings of his childhood. Most patients, to some extent, want to obtain in the transference those urges and wishes which they could not renounce in childhood. I have also observed that many patients sense whether the analyst is faking positive feelings toward them or whether his feelings are sincere.[33]

(One can sense here a basis for Weiss's rapport with Alexander's own approach.) Weiss thought he had succeeded in helping with this patient's recovery partly because Weiss had genuinely liked him, despite the patient's imaginary fear that Weiss had preferred other patients to him.

When Weiss wrote to Freud in 1922 about a therapeutic failure with a young physician, Freud was reassuring in terms that were uniquely characteristic of Freud's special approach. If this analysis had been successful, the patient intended to become an analyst, and would have been Weiss's first "analytic colleague in Trieste." But the patient was in contact "with other colleagues, opponents of psychoanalysis, and to them he revealed what we discussed in his analytic sessions...Eventually he quit treatment." Freud wrote Weiss:

> Don't take it so seriously! An analyst must expect such small accidents, especially in a hostile environment. Consider furthermore that, regretfully, only a few patients are worth the trouble we spend on them, so that we are not allowed to have a therapeutic attitude, but we must be glad to have learned something in every case. A patient who always talks to others about his analysis aims from the beginning to expose analysis.[34]

Freud's same moralism was implicitly reflected also in Anna Freud's own writings; for them both an analysis was an ethical moral ideal. She once proposed for "impulsive" adults that "you would treat the patient by a mixed method, giving him as much pure analysis as he can stand and for the rest children's analysis—because, owing to his infantile nature, he would merit nothing better." And she once wrote to her friend Eva Rosenfeld, embarking on analysis with Freud: "You will see that being good and being in analysis finally amount to the same thing."[35]

Another case of Weiss's, "one of my most interesting patients, Mr. F. G.," after an apparently successful treatment with Weiss that overcame a severe depression and lack of heterosexual feelings, went to visit Freud, who saw him for a couple of sessions; Freud considered him cured and even invited him to a meeting of the Vienna Psychoanalytic Society. Freud often helped transform former patients into followers. Later this patient—who had had a recurrence of bronchial asthma during treatment—did badly, and according to Weiss,

> blamed the analytic treatment for his terrible situation. He blamed the analytic procedure for his asthma. And in a way he was right. Had the analysis not freed his strong attachment to his mother and to women in general, he would have remained depressed but he would not have suffered from asthma.

(Weiss continued to think in terms of how the "treatment" of problems could expose worse difficulties.) Once Freud had heard that the case had not gone as well as he and Weiss had initially thought, Freud consoled Weiss with the observation that "the admission of one's own interest arouses in the patient a need for revenge." Such reasoning, for Freud, justified analytic aloofness. "How the situation will end cannot be predicted safely. Let us hope that you will keep the upper hand. It is a therapeutic *pis aller* [last resource] that the patient gets well by scolding his physician and the analysis...."

But then in 1924 the patient wrote Freud "a long registered letter," reproaching him for supposedly having written his *The Ego and the Id* as a justification for the failure of the patient's own particular analysis. Once Freud had heard this way directly from the patient, he was in "no doubt about the diagnosis 'paranoia querulans.'"

> the letter is quite impertinent, and aggressive, and without practical point...Many patients have cursed their way to health. Or you have had the bad luck to run into a latent paranoia and through the cure of his neurosis you may have freed a more serious sickness. This may happen to each of us occasionally and there is no protection against it.[36]

(Only four years later another disciple of Freud's, Ruth Mack Brunswick, would make a similar observation about Freud's famous patient the "Wolf-Man," after he had been later treated by herself: "It may be that the first analysis [with Freud] robbed him of the usual neurotic modes of solution. One may ask oneself if the patient was perhaps always latently paranoid."[37]) It is reminiscent of Freud's early case of a "cured" agoraphobia that broke out into schizophrenia, which was then "treated" by re-imposing the agoraphobia. On the other hand, it can well be that psychoanalytic thinking offered too many rationalizations for therapeutic failure. And it was part of Weiss's humaneness that he concluded from Freud's teachings that "the need of some patients to find in the transference satisfaction of urges and wishes which remained unsatisfied in childhood may apply also to negative, hostile transference."[38]

After years of experience with Freud's approach to patients, Weiss was convinced that Freud's idea that the analyst should present himself as a "blank screen" to the patient was "a mistake." Freud "was not so" neutral himself. As much as Freud could show "great consideration for human weaknesses," he remained strongly opposed to anti-social and criminal tendencies in people; Freud was so lacking in objectivity about his own "counter-transferences" to patients that that was why, according to Weiss, Freud scarcely ever wrote about the phenomena of bias in analysts; the very term "counter-transference" implies that the analyst's reaction to patients is a genuine response to clinical material, rather than something initiated originally from within the analyst's own mental world.[39] Weiss insisted that one must distinguish between reality and transference. The analyst's positive feelings for a patient, for example if he is honest and upright, is a realistic factor to be taken into account; just as all the emotional reactions in analysts themselves are not of a transference nature, referable to some past conflicts, so all a patient's criticisms of the analyst's behavior are not to be written off as simply "negative transference," but can have a realistic basis in therapeutic errors. An interesting recent literature has arisen on the whole subject of the therapeutic functions of the real relationship in psychoanalysis.[40]

Freud had more than once made the point to the kindly Weiss about the bad consequences of giving into the analyst's own interest in the patient. Weiss had in 1934 written to Freud about Concetta Forzano, the daughter of a cabinet minister of Mussolini's. (In different publications Weiss referred to her as "Miss N. N." and also "Ethel.") Freud began writing about her with the utmost restraint: "It is very difficult to assume the responsibility in such a case. Therefore I must expressly refuse to advise you and I will tell you only how the case looks to me and what I would do according to my experience, without putting you under any obligation." Freud tried to warn Weiss against therapeutic ambitiousness, in declaring that he thought she "will probably not give in as long as she can guess how much her recovery means to you." Weiss had allowed her, when she complained about having to lie on the couch, to sit on a chair facing him; Weiss thought it would help her to overcome some of her negative feelings. Freud was cautiously disapproving:

> These patients are very dangerous, even more so when they are intelligent, because they do not use their intelligence to control their passions but in order to serve them...[S]he knows exactly what special importance her recovery has for your case. Furthermore, that she succeeded in getting a great concession from your part; I mean, you should not have allowed her to exchange the prescribed position for one more pleasant to her...The underlying rule naturally is that the analyst should not come forth when the patient withdraws, instead he himself should hold back. I will be pleased to hear, however, that you have found a satisfactory solution in your case.[41]

Freud had originally sounded cautious at first in print recommending the use of the couch, and asserted that "this technique is the only one suited to my individuality"; other analysts might be differently inclined.[42] In keeping with this tentativeness, Freud had overlooked Jung's own ways of proceeding, but by the 1920s was capable of complaining also about Brill's not making enough use of the couch. Freud could make a temporary exception for the poet H.D. in 1933, but not for long.[43]

As orthodox an analyst as he sounds here supervising Weiss, Freud, with this particular patient, also recommended a temporary interruption of the treatment with a promise to resume after several months; such a hiatus was a therapeutic maneuver which was not ever included in Freud's formal written technical recommendations. Weiss nonetheless by now felt able to introduce some of his own "concessions" to the standardized model of analytic treatment, even those "compromises" Freud might have disapproved of. So he did not interrupt the treatment. Weiss not only permitted this formerly agoraphobic patient to sit in the chair "sometimes," but "since she was often afraid to leave the house, I offered to accompany her on the street, and she reacted to this very favorably."[44] According to Weiss, she made good progress, was free of her earlier hysterical seizures, and was married and pregnant at the time he emigrated to the States.

Freud had interpreted "Ethel's" hysterical screams as repetitions of her mother's crises during childbirth; but Weiss instead concluded that they were not a historical remnant of a memory associated with the birth of a younger sibling, but rather an existential terror because she was afraid of losing her ego through disintegrating. Reconstructions of the past were, in a sense, Freud's greatest strength and enabled him to set going much later investigation of earliest childhood; but such a long-term inspiration, in this case a hypothesis about possible memories of childbirth, could be at odds with realistic therapeutic needs. Weiss felt that "changes" in Concetta's "environment awoke in her the frightening feeling of internal changes," and therefore he offered her more support and comfort. Weiss's indebtedness to Federn's ego psychology was enduring, and in later years Weiss tried to rethink the significance of this particular woman's difficulties.[45] Although he was, like other early followers of Freud's, committed to the theoretical significance of his therapeutic endeavors, Weiss remained unusually dedicated to what could be learned from concrete clinical realities.

Notes

1. "Recommendations to Physicians Practising Psychoanalysis," *Standard Edition*, Vol. 12 (London: Hogarth Press, 1953-74), p. 119.
2. Roazen, *Freud and His Followers* (New York: Alfred A. Knopf, 1974), pp. 145-53.
3. "Mourning and Melancholia," *Standard Edition*, Vol. 14, p. 247.
4. *The Complete Correspondence of Sigmund Freud and Karl Abraham 1907-1925* (London: Karmac, 2002), pp. 281-84.
5. Weiss, *Sigmund Freud as a Consultant: Recollections of a Pioneer in Psychoanalysis*, with an introduction by Martin Grotjahn (New York: Intercontinental Medical Book Corporation, 1970; New Brunswick, NJ: Transaction Publishers, 1991), p. 27.
6. I remain indebted to Dr. Sonia Buglione for first alerting me to Bruno Veneziani's identity in the psychoanalytic literature. See also John Gatt-Rutter, *Italo Svevo: A Double Life* (Oxford:Clarendon Press, 1988), p. 305.
7. Livia Veneziani Svevo, *Memoir of Italo Svevo* (Evanston, IL: The Marlboro Press/Northwestern University Press, 2001), pp. 5, 57.
8. Weiss, *Sigmund Freud as a Consultant*, op. cit., pp. 23-27.
9. P. N. Furbank, *Italo Svevo: The Man and the Writer* (London: Secker and Warburg, 1966), pp. 106-07.
10. Livia Veneziani Svevo, *Memoir of Italo Svevo*, pp. 74-75.
11. Victor Brombert, "Italo Svevo: The Paradoxes of the Anti-Hero," *Yale Review*, Vol. 82, No. 1 (1994), pp. 70-71.
12. Furbank, *Italo Svevo*, p. 179.
13. Elizabeth Mahler-Schachter, "Svevo, Trieste, and the Vienna Circle: Zeno's Analyst Analysed," *European Studies Review*, vol. 12, no. 1 (Jan. 1982), p. 51.
14. See Crane Brinton, *A Decade of Revolution 1789-1799* (New York: Harper & Brothers, 1934), p. 104.

15. David J. Lynn, "Freud's Analysis of A.B., A Psychotic Man, 1925-1930," *The Journal of the American Academy of Psychoanalysis*, Vol. 21, No. 1 (Spring 1993), p. 69. See also Alex Beam, *Gracefully Insane: The Rise and Fall of America's Premier Mental Hospital* (New York: Public Affairs, 2001), pp. 106-16, 184-87.
16. Weiss, *Sigmund Freud as a Consultant*, pp. 27-28.
17. Carl M. Grossman and Sylvia Grossman, *The Wild Analyst: The Life and Work of Georg Groddeck* (New York: George Braziller, 1965); Georg Groddeck, *The Book of the It* (New York: Vintage, 1961); *Ferenczi-Groddeck Correspondence 1921-33*, ed. Christopher Fortune (London: Open Gate Press, 2002).
18. Georg Groddeck, *The Meaning of Illness* (London: Hogarth Press, 1970), p. 82.
19. Weiss, *Sigmund Freud as a Consultant*, p. 28-29.
20. Paul Roazen, *How Freud Worked: First-Hand Accounts of Patients* (Northvale, NJ: Jason Aronson, 1995), ch. 6, pp. 143-65.
21. *Letters of Sigmund Freud 1873-1939*, ed. Ernst L. Freud (London: Hogarth Press, 1961), pp. 419-20. See also Roazen, *How Freud Worked*, ch. 9, pp. 231-55, and Roazen, *The Historiography of Psychoanalysis* (New Brunswick, NJ: Transaction Publishers, 2000), pp. 145-49.
22. Paul Roazen, *Helene Deutsch: A Psychoanalyst's Life* (New Brunswick, NJ: Transaction Publishers, 1992), pp. 266-67.
23. *Analyzing Freud: Letters of H.D., Bryher, and Their Circle*, ed. Susan Stanford Friedman (New York: New Directions, 2002).
24. *The Complete Correspondence of Karl Abraham and Sigmund Freud 1907-25*, p. 284.
25. "Eissler Interview," p. 24.
26. Letter from Edoardo Weiss to Jones, June 30, 1956, "Commentary."
27. Weiss, *Sigmund Freud as a Consultant*, p. 34
28. Ibid., pp. 35-36.
29. Ibid., p. 36.
30. *The Complete Letters of Sigmund Freud and Karl Abraham*, p. 13.
31. Weiss, *Sigmund Freud as a Consultant*, pp. 31-32.
32. Ibid., p. 35. See also Siegfried Bernfeld, "On Psychoanalytic Training," *Psychoanalytic Quarterly*, Vol. 31, No. 4 (1962), pp. 453-82.
33. Weiss, *Sigmund Freud as a Consultant*, p. 42-43.
34. Ibid., p. 37.
35. Anna Freud, *The Psychoanalytic Treatment of Children*, translated by Nancy Procter-Gregg (London: Imago Publishing Co., 1946), pp. 51-52; Peter Heller, *Anna Freud's Letters to Eva Rosenfeld*, translated by Mary Weigand (Madison, CT, International Universities Press, 1992), p. 112.
36. Weiss, *Sigmund Freud as a Consultant*, pp. 44-50.
37. *The Wolf-Man by the Wolf-Man*, ed. Muriel Gardiner (New York: Basic Books, 1971), p. 305.
38. Weiss, *Sigmund Freud as a Consultant*, p.49.
39. I am indebted for this point to Dr. Leston Havens.

40. Arthur S. Couch, "The Therapeutic Functions of the Real Relationship in Psychoanalysis," *The Psychoanalytic Study of the Child*, Vol. 54 (New Haven, CT: Yale University Press, 1999), pp.130-68.
41. Weiss, *Sigmund Freud as a Consultant*, pp. 74-78.
42. Roazen, *Freud and His Followers*, pp. 122-23.
43. *Analyzing Freud: Letters of H.D., Bryher, and Their Circle*, p. 59.
44. Weiss, *Sigmund Freud as a Consultant*, pp. 74-78.
45. Weiss, *Agoraphobia in the Light of Ego Psychology* (New York: Grune and Stratton, 1964), pp. 54-63.

9

Politics

In the winter of 1925, a well-known psychiatrist in Turin, Professor Enrico Morselli (1852-1929),[1] had written to Weiss to learn about Freud's concepts and his form of therapy. He asked for information about Freud as if he would be favorably inclined. Weiss cooperated in sending him "a long exchange of letters," and out of "gratitude" Morselli, to show his "appreciation," invited Weiss to present a paper at an Italian psychiatric convention to be held September 24-27, 1925 in Trieste. Weiss thought his presentation had gone well and been favorably received, except that "at the end of the session Morselli himself wanted to close the discussion by criticizing Freud's analysis, distorting his concepts, without considering all the explanations I had given him in our long correspondence. I was shocked at this hypocritical and false attitude, as were a number of the psychiatrists."[2] Weiss felt betrayed by Morselli, in a complicated sort of double-cross, and Weiss concluded that Morselli was an ambitious, dishonest person. With Levi-Bianchini as an ally, Weiss was entitled to feel that his position in Italy was "terrible."

Morselli could propose the old idea that dreams were merely the result of physical stimulation. Earlier, during World War I, writers like E. Tanzi and E. Lugaro had published articles against German psychiatry, using Freud as an example, ignoring that the German professions were largely against him. Following Freud's splits with Adler and Jung, Tanzi and Lugaro could anticipate, according to how Weiss summarized their work, that these dissensions heralded the onset of the complete destruction of psychoanalysis; Weiss thought there was "no evidence that Lugaro had ever seen a patient who had undergone psychoanalytic treatment," and offered the following quotation as "representative" of his 1917 criticism of psychoanalysis:

> The greatest errors of the psychoanalytic method are amassed in the interpretation of dreams. In this investigation a leaden preoccupation with sexual perversions is obligatory....In the psychological hermeneutic everything is clear, every dream image has the value of a precise symbol; climbing stairs means having sexual intercourse; seeing the tower of Pisa is the same as doubting one's sexual impotency; a wardrobe, a stove, a snuffbox symbolize the female body! We would not have dwelled on this argument if such doctrinary lucubrations did not arouse an interest that, in many respects, impresses us as pathological. But the infatuation of the neophyte will pass and in the psychoanalytic church there are already schisms, precursors of decay.[3]

Against such an Italian backdrop, repeated in a 1923 third edition of the same book, Freud wrote to Weiss on January 23, 1926:

> A few days ago I received Morselli's two volume "La Psicanalisi." It is completely without value, the only value is its undoubted proof that he is a donkey. It contains numerous large and small mistakes, the most stupid arguments, old and new, is written with little knowledge of the literature and obviously without any expert knowledge. Furthermore, it is covered by a layer of false courtesy, as used to be characteristic for the Katzelmacher in old Austria.

"Katzelmacher" was a traditional Hapsburg disparaging expression for Italians; Freud, once having used it and knowing Weiss's Italian nationalist commitments, immediately put in a parenthetical apology: "(I hope that your patriotic sentiments do not take offense at this reminiscence.)" Freud was commissioning Weiss to undertake necessary polemical warfare: "I expect you to assume the detailed critique for our journal. I ask you not to spare him any unpleasant truth in this case."[4] A few days later Freud wrote Sandor Ferenczi about Morselli's "two thick volumes": "Manure and rubbish!"[5]

Weiss, before having heard from Freud, had already starting writing "devastating" criticisms of Morselli; and so he undertook the assignment from Freud "with great pleasure," publishing a review both in Levi-Bianchini's Italian journal and in German for the official Freudian *Psychoanalytische Zeitschrift*. By June 3, Freud could send Weiss his appreciative thanks:

> Many thanks for having accomplished this unpleasant assignment. It could not have been a pleasure for you. Your critique is harsh but certainly not undeserved. It is a miserable piece of work. At one point you have even spared the author. I mean, where his undignified, repellent hunting for popularity among the Italian public comes to the surface. Small changes and some shortening will probably be done with your permission by the editors whom I have notified of your work today. I am glad that you have shown yourself to be courageous and honest, as always....

Morselli was so "enraged" by Weiss's Italian and German criticism that he wrote "a long insulting article" about Weiss in a psychiatric journal. "He also lied about the explanation I had given him on how one proceeds in psychoanalytic therapy." Part of Morselli's "revenge" consisted in reasoning that since transference means a patient wanting to be kissed, that meant Weiss kissed his patients. Weiss sent Freud a copy of the issue in which Morselli's piece appeared, and Freud answered Weiss:

> I have learned from Morselli's stupid and malicious prattle and return the number to you. I do not doubt at all that he falsified your statements as he did mine. You are right not to answer him. If you should ever in any connection want to let him know that I approve your criticism completely, I leave that to you.[6]

Unknown to Weiss, however, within weeks of Freud's having received Morselli's two volumes, which arrived also with a pamphlet of Morselli's on Zionism, and after Freud had first asked Weiss to write a critique, Freud had himself written flatteringly to Morselli. Eissler never brought up Freud's own letter to Morselli with Weiss, but I did, and Weiss—who had not noticed its existence before—subsequently reprinted it, almost without comment, in his own book of Freud letters.

On Feb. 18, 1926 Freud had written Morselli:

> While reading your important work on psychoanalysis I noticed with regret that you cannot accept our youthful science without great reservations, and I have to comfort myself with the divergence of opinion inevitable in such difficult topics as well as with the certainty that your book will contribute a great deal towards arousing the interest of your compatriots for psychoanalysis.

Although Freud and Morselli, almost exact contemporaries, presumably shared in the same Old World manners, one has to wonder whether Morselli ever guessed Freud's true feelings about his work on psychoanalysis, especially since Freud went on to write so positively about Morselli's piece on Zionism.

> But your pamphlet on the Zionist question I was able to read without mixed feelings, with unreserved approval, and I was pleased to see with what sympathy, humaneness and understanding you were able to choose your point of view concerning the matter which has been distorted by human passions. I feel as though obliged to send you my personal thanks for it.[7]

Now Freud's own relationship to Zionism is a complicated issue. Theodor Herzl and his work come up repeatedly, if sometimes anonymously, in *The Interpretation of Dreams*. Freud was proud to have become one of the directors of the Hebrew University in Jerusalem. Orthodox Jews there remained so offended by Theodor Reik's *Ritual: Four Psychoanalytic Studies,*[8] originally published in 1919 with a preface by Freud and dealing with Kol Nidre and the shofar, along with the couvade and the puberty rites of "savages" as well as neurotics, that they objected to the creation of a chair of psychoanalysis. Shortly after some 1929 Arab riots in Hebron, when Freud was asked publicly to express his sympathies with the Jewish national movement, he wrote a letter that for many years was "hidden from the public and was explicitly retrieved from the Jewish National Library and requested to be sent back to Vienna."

> Whoever wishes to influence a mass needs to have something sonorous and enthusiastic to say, and my sober assessment of Zionism does not permit this. I certainly have the greatest sympathy for voluntary efforts, am proud of our university in Jerusalem, and am happy that our settlements are thriving. But, on the other hand, I do not believe that Palestine can ever be a Jewish state, and that either the Christian or Islamic world will ever be ready to place their holy places under Jewish guardianship. It would seem more sensible to me to found a Jewish fatherland on historically untroubled soil—though I realize that such a rational goal would never have gained the enthusiasm of the masses and the collaboration of the wealthy. I also regrettably admit that the fanaticism of our fellow Jews, estranged as it is from reality, bears its share of responsibility for the rise of mistrust among the Arabs. I can conjure up absolutely no sympathy for that misguided piety which renders a piece of Herod's wall a national relic and aggravates

> the feelings of the native population on its account. Judge for yourself if, possessing such a critical stance, I am the proper person to offer solace to a people shaken in its unfounded hope.

What Freud had to say about "a piece of Herod's wall" would remain unknown for over half a century. But the reactions to Freud's *Moses and Monotheism*, in which Freud considered both Moses as well as his doctrine as Egyptian, struck Zionists at the time as a betrayal.[9] Yet part of the reason that Freud had needed a Gentile like Jung as his "crown prince" was because Freud sought to use psychoanalysis to undermine Christian culture; Freud's Augustinian-like reasoning, and his reliance on dream life, could be understood at a roundabout way to use Christianity against itself.[10]

It may be as hard to untangle Freud's views on Zionism as it can be to follow his outlook on Morselli. Morselli's volumes on psychoanalysis and his article on Zionism were linked together, yet Freud scarcely allowed himself to show displeasure in public: "I am not sure that your opinion," he wrote Morselli, "which looks upon psychoanalysis as a direct product of the Jewish mind, is correct, but if it is I wouldn't be ashamed." Any such linkage between the origins of psychoanalysis and Judaism, coming from someone like Jung, would be deemed in print by Freud as straightforward anti-Semitism. Yet with Morselli, Freud sounds forbearing:

> Although I have been alienated from the religion of my forebears for a long time, I have never lost the feeling of solidarity with my people and realize with satisfaction that you call yourself a pupil of a man of my race, the great Lombroso.
>
> In the past I wouldn't have hesitated to ask your permission to visit you on my next trip to Italy. Unfortunately I cannot consider travelling at the moment.[11]

Freud, who first got cancer of the jaw in 1923, which in the end was to preclude his further Italian travels, can hardly have been unacquainted with the "false courtesy" that he attributed to Italians by the word "Katzelmacher." Until the time I first interviewed Weiss in 1965 he had proudly cherished Freud's January 23, 1926 letter to him that had said of Morselli's study: "It is completely without value, the only value is its undoubted proof that he is a donkey."

Weiss was naïve enough to be "shocked" at the "contradictory behavior" when I showed him Freud's own letter to Morselli that was in such contrast to Freud's convictions as expressed privately to Weiss. Jones used to like to sentimentalize what he called Freud's "flawless integrity,"[12] the supposed complete identity between what Freud said and believed. (In 1932 an American psychologist, Joseph Jastrow, wrote a book called *The House that Freud Built*. Freud sent a letter to Smith Ely Jelliffe that Jastrow had written him to say that he hoped Freud "would not take his criticism amiss. In my reply I assured him I would not, which sounds polite but is actually an insult, since it amounts to saying: I don't care in the least what you may write about me." Freud wanted Jelliffe to "chastise" Jastrow publicly.[13]) Again and again, Jones talked about Freud's probity and honesty, his passion for uncompromising truthfulness, his courage and hatred of hypocrisy. Yet the contrast between what Freud wrote Weiss about Morselli's work, and what Freud sent Morselli directly, sounds more like the typical insincerities of a successful man of the world.[14] Masud Khan, in writing to Anna Freud in 1970, had noticed the potential problem here:

> Professor Freud's letter to Morselli himself...of course is written with a certain courtesy and generosity that the letter to Weiss clearly negates. I do not know what Dr. Weiss's intention was in juxtaposing these two letters. Perhaps today it is very difficult for people to understand that in public life there used to be a tradition of civility and courtesy and it should not be mistaken for any other motivations.[15]

In behalf of psychoanalysis, Freud knew how to be a good moderate-seeming politician, although at the same time an intransigent leader of his "cause." Freud could write praising obituaries of both Ferenczi and Tausk, while privately expressing acutely disparaging feelings; Freud also publicly honored Jones while at the same time writing a letter indicating how much he disliked him personally.[16] Weiss may not have realized at the time how Freud was leaving him with the burden of dealing with Morselli. But Weiss was always aware of the problem Freud had created for him in Italy because of encouraging Levi-Bianchini. In a letter of September 30, 1926, Freud implicitly acknowledged to Weiss that Levi-Bianchini's so-called psychoanalytic society was fraudulent, but Freud wanted Weiss's cooperation in tolerating it for the time being:

> one must accept the way it is. After all, it happens frequently that the form appears before the content, and I am glad that you don't now intend to destroy this form. Let us hope that this form in time will be filled with content, and when this happens, it will be your accomplishment and to your merit. I think about Levi-Bianchini exactly as you do. I have always judged his weaknesses and his good sides as you do in your letters.[17]

Freud had written Levi-Bianchini on June 16, 1925 to congratulate him on the foundation of the "new" society. (Weiss never mentioned to me that Levi-Bianchini had become an elected member of the Vienna Psychoanalytic Society.) In his edition of his letters from Freud, Weiss in part conceded that "Levi-Bianchini deserved Freud's recognition. He was defiant of the opinions of the established psychiatric authorities who rejected psychoanalysis, and he had a propagandist spirit."[18] And Levi-Bianchini had been prescient in predicting as early as 1923 that in Italy "Freud, thrown out the front door of psychiatry, will come in through the back door of the intellectual world (philosophy, psychology, literature)."[19] But one can guess Weiss's annoyance at Jones in Marienbad (1937) mentioning that although Weiss's journal had been politically suppressed, Levi-Bianchini had assured Jones "that there was ample opportunity for publication" in his own periodical.[20] Weiss was entitled to be offended when Levi-Bianchini, just as Weiss was in January 1939 leaving for America, made sure to give a framed copy of Freud's 1925 letter to him to remind Weiss who founded Italian psychoanalysis.

Morselli's being in Italy made him part of Weiss's psychoanalytic territory, and in the same letter about Levi-Bianchini's "form" being all right even if the "content" left something to be desired, Freud continued to endorse Weiss's critique of Morselli: "Your criticism of Morselli is exactly what we wished. Where it appears harsh, Morselli deserves this harshness." On December 14, 1926 Freud returned to Morselli; when Freud felt embattled his polemical style rose to the occasion:

> It was enjoyable and entertaining to read your detailed critique of Morselli. Nothing in it is unjust and he deserved it. It would be humanly interesting to learn whether he has always been such a bum or whether he has permitted himself to become that way only under the influence of senility.[21]

It should come as no surprise that Weiss thought that Freud could be "very bitter and sarcastic towards enemies," but only unexpected that he allowed this comment to come out in speaking with the loyalist Eissler.[22]

However Weiss may have struggled in his career in Trieste, Freud had assured him, in connection with an Italian translation Weiss had done in 1922: "I hope it will soon be worth your while since the interest now has strengthened so much in France and Spain."[23] And the next year Freud had written him: "Have no doubt that there is a future for psychoanalysis in Italy also. You only have to wait for a good time."[24] (In 1909 Freud had similarly encouraged Abraham in Germany: "As you are the only one in Berlin, it should work out for you even better; it will come to pass."[25]) Prince Metternich at the Congress of Vienna had scathingly referred to Italy as "a geographical expression"; and as it was observed even after Italian unification, "though Italy was made, it nevertheless remained to make Italians."[26] Weiss had been tempted to emigrate from Italy in 1927, when he resigned from the Trieste psychiatric hospital because "at that time everyone in an official position was obliged to join the Fascist party," which Weiss "refused to do." Freud wrote back:

> Your letter has given me deep concern since I did not suspect at all that you had material difficulties. You yourself know how little advice from an outsider can help as a rule. Therefore I am glad that you have spoken with me about your situation and I will tell you gladly what I think. You cannot decide on the basis of the city from which the most patients turn towards me, because I have almost no requests from Italy. Perhaps at most from Trieste, which is the result of your influence. As much as I know of Italian cities, Milan seems to me also the liveliest and I would say the most European, the most suitable place. Unfavorable information should never keep you away because one gets that everywhere, one must try and create the need through his own presence.
>
> Translations and analytic teaching may wait until the time is right. I think that the analytical wave which now goes high in Paris will reach Italy sometime in the future. I can only advise you against emigration. One is unwelcome everywhere and it is especially difficult for a foreigner. I have been informed by a lady of great influence about conditions in France (Paris). She says it is necessary to repeat all the examinations—this is an absolute hindrance. If you ask Jones, you will hear only complaints that the analysts in his group do not have enough to do. Incomplete knowledge of the language is the least forgivable in England.

Ophuijsen in The Hague has threatened to emigrate for years, I have always advised him against it, and he is still at home. One never has better prospect for finally succeeded than in one's own country.

Weiss was still in Trieste, technically Italian but becoming more isolated than before World War I. Freud concluded: "I know these are especially unfavorable times and times in which one is inclined to despair. I hope that both will pass for you and that you will remain as the legitimate representative of analysis in Italy."[27] Just before Weiss settled in Rome in 1930, Freud commended him for a translation: "You are the right, enduring pioneer."[28]

In contrast to what Freud before World War I had regarded as "the absence of any deep-rooted scientific tradition in America," as well as its surface popularity there, he held that it was "for this reason the ancient centers of culture, where the greatest resistance has been displayed, must be the scene of the decisive struggle over psychoanalysis."[29] So Spain, France, and Italy remained linked in Freud's mind as Catholic countries he hoped eventually to win over. Weiss therefore was an instrument of Freud's cause.

When Weiss was prepared to publish as a book his 1930 series of lectures on psychoanalysis that he gave at the invitation of the Trieste Medical Association, Freud agreed to "gladly write the desired introduction. It is a pleasure to have a chance to do something for you. Please tell me approximately what I should write." Freud wrote again to Weiss: "I will gladly give you warm words of recommendation. You certainly deserve it." Freud knew how to dispense patronage, and it was his daughter Anna's practice too to write prefaces to articles and books of favored students. The terms of Freud's praise for Weiss's book were expressed in sentences characteristic of Freud's style of writing:

> The author of these lectures, my friend and pupil Dr. Edoardo Weiss, has expressed a wish that I should send his work on its way with a few words of recommendation. In doing so I am fully aware that such a recommendation is superfluous. The work speaks for itself. All who know how to appreciate the seriousness of a scientific endeavor, how to value the honesty of an investigator who does not seek to belittle or deny the difficulties, and how to take pleasure in the skill of a teacher who brings light into darkness and order into chaos by his exposition, must form a high estimate of this book and share my hope that it will awaken among cultivated and learned circles in Italy a lasting interest in the young science of psychoanalysis.[30]

Freud did not often send books forth with such endorsements, and I think his praise for Weiss belies Anna Freud's later attempt to belittle Weiss. Weiss modestly told Eissler that he had the feeling that the book itself did not merit such praise, but that Freud had felt guilty because of having been responsible for publicly associating him with Levi-Bianchini in that 1923 footnote to Freud's *On the History of the Psychoanalytic Movement*. Weiss's *Elementi di Psicoanalisis* went into three editions until it was banned by the Fascists in 1938; in Germany, Freud's own books, along with other psychoanalytic texts, had been burned starting in 1933. Once Weiss started his psychoanalytic Society in Rome in 1931, because of this book of Weiss's he began to attract students.

Weiss, like Freud and other early analysts, was intrigued by occult experiences, and given Weiss's standing in Freud's movement he had to be concerned about how far this interest of Weiss's might lead. Weiss had written Freud about one medium's telepathic performances, and on April 24, 1932 Freud replied at length, interested but also anxious that Weiss might have been taken in by a "cheat," and worried that Weiss's associating occultism publicly to psychoanalysis would be damaging to the "cause":

> I am, it is true, prepared to believe that behind all so-called occult phenomena lies something new and important: the fact of thought-transference, i.e., the transferring of psychical processes through space to other people. I know of proofs of this observation made in daylight and am thinking of expressing my opinion publicly about it. Naturally it would be unfavorable for the part you play as the pioneer of psychoanalysis in Italy were you to proclaim yourself at the same time a partisan of occultism.[31]

Freud had earlier defended his conception of infantile sexuality in similar terms; he thought he had "discovered" material that could be described as "facts" but which others would repudiate as unsavory. One of Freud's polemical accusations against Jung had been that he had repudiated the so-called facts of infantile sexuality; and Jung shared the conviction that his own contributions were matters of "fact" rather than conceptual. "Transference" was something else that Freud considered factual. Many historians have written as if Freud had "discovered" the unconscious, or psychoanalysis itself, instead of proposing that Freud's real achievement lay in his having created a new way of thinking about things. Had Freud adopted a different methodology of science it might have made it easier to disagree with him.

Freud's belief in the "fact" of thought-transference (telepathy) was long known to Weiss, as Freud more than once published on the occult,[32] and Weiss once again wrote Freud about Weiss's further interest in para-psychological feats. Freud felt he had to clarify to Weiss the distinction between Freud's receptivity about the occult and his dubiousness on the reliability of mediums: "A psychoanalyst's refraining from taking part publicly in occult studies is a purely practical measure, and only a temporary one, not at all an expression on principle." Contemporaries of Weiss's in analysis would have been familiar with the idea that they were supposed to be "elastic" in practice but firm in principle.

> Contemptuous rejection of these studies without any experience of them would really be to imitate the deplorable example of our opponents. In this matter I think just as you do. Furthermore to take flight, in a cowardly fashion and behind the shelter of disdain, from the allegedly "supernatural" shows very little confidence in the trustworthiness of our scientific *Weltanschauung*.
>
> The medium business, however, is a disagreeable chapter. The unquestionable deceptions on the part of mediums, the simpleminded and tricky nature of their performances, the difficulties of testing them in the peculiar conditions chosen by them, the obvious impossibilities of many of their claims—all that calls for the utmost caution. There must surely be better ways of showing what is real in the occult. The techniques used until now are too reminiscent of the traveling and currency restrictions with their later added senseless improvements which however do not work any better.

Freud, living in Vienna then, knew at first hand about evading currency restrictions. (In Italy Weiss and his wife were unable to prepare themselves financially for their eventual migration, although the forced sale to a Gentile of Weiss's father's factory netted some English pounds for the family.) Freud's open-mindedness about "what is real in the occult" distressed a skeptic like Jones, but was interpreted by him as part of the receptivity to the new that allowed Freud to take something like dreaming seriously in the first place. While writing to Weiss about the problem of occultism, Freud was also passing along to Weiss how he had taken the side of Weiss's new Italian group within the International Psychoanalytic Association.

> I have recommended to Dr. Eitingon the prompt acceptance of your group very soon, with the argument that the leader vouches for all others. The argument that the by-laws of the IPA demands that all members must have been analyzed themselves remains, however, in force.[33]

In the next year, Freud had given Weiss some recommendations about reorganizing an article about psychoanalysis for the Italian *Enciclopedia*, a publication considered "huge and impressive" while "free of political slant."[34]

One of the last letters from Freud to Weiss came on November 1, 1935, and on a subject at least as explosive as the occult; for as we touched on Weiss had been tempted to analyze his older son, Emilio, supposedly for purposes of training, and Weiss had first turned to Freud for consulting advice. Emilio had already gently, and without hard feelings, put aside the idea of the analysis. But it was in the course of what Weiss took to be Freud's attempt to discourage him from analyzing the son, that Freud had put into writing the startling news that he had actually analyzed Anna Freud: "Concerning the analysis of your hopeful son, that is certainly a ticklish business. With a younger bother it might be done more easily." (Weiss younger brother Ottocaro in fact went to Nunberg during World War I.)

> With one's own daughter I succeeded well. There are special difficulties and doubts with a son.
>
> Not that I really would warn you against a danger; obviously everything depends on the two people and their relationship to each other. You know the difficulties. It would not surprise me if you were successful in spite of them. It is difficult for an outsider to decide. I would not advise you to do it and have no right to forbid it.[35]

Other analysts of that first generation (such as Brill and Melanie Klein) did undertake, like Freud himself, to analyze children of their own, although I do not know if Weiss was aware of it at the time. Later he told me it had been "very indiscreet" of Freud to mention his analysis of Anna in a letter; he thought she would not have liked it. Weiss said that he did not tell anybody about it then. Freud had been free in criticizing the technical practices of other analysts, such as Ferenczi: "What one does in the way of technique one must also represent publicly."[36] Analyzing Anna himself reflected, Weiss thought, an oedipal attachment on Freud's part, and it was "a mistake."

In my experience few analysts, despite their natural protectiveness about Freud's reputation, have considered enough his awareness about how any other analyst might possibly have injured Anna. In justifying his own early metaphor of analysis as like surgery, Freud liked to talk about its capacity to heal being tied with the possibility of its doing harm. Presumably another analyst would have had to try to promote Anna's autonomy, which might have meant attempting to wean her from dependency on her father; it is hard to imagine any of Freud's followers being eager to undertake such a perilous mission, even if Anna had consented to having another analyst after Freud himself. Rumors circulated for years that Anna had chosen to go to Lou Andreas-Salomé, and Weiss himself seemed to share in that legend; but Anna tried to make it clear that her father had been her only analyst. As we have seen, even with Masud Khan she maintained studied silence.

On the occasion of Freud's eightieth birthday in 1936, Weiss arranged to dedicate an issue of Levi-Bianchini's journal in Italy to him, and the collection subsequently appeared as a book. Weiss received a formal card from Freud thanking him for having participated in his birthday celebration, and also these personal words: "Under your leadership the analysts of Italy have given especially impressive testimony of their belonging to the analytic community on this occasion. The name Edoardo Weiss assures a rich future."[37]

Notes

1. Henri F. Ellenberger, *The Discovery of the Unconscious: The History and Evolution of Dynamic Psychiatry* (New York: Basic Books, 1970), pp. 755, 782, 847.
2. Edoardo Weiss, *Sigmund Freud as a Consultant: Recollections of a Pioneer in Psychoanalysis*, with an introduction by Martin Grotjahn (New York: Intercontinental Medical Book Corporation, 1970; New Brunswick, NJ: Transaction Publishers, 1991), pp. 51-52.
3. Ibid., pp. 7-8.
4. Ibid., p. 52.
5. *The Correspondence of Sigmund Freud and Sandor Ferenczi*, Vol. 3, *1920-1933*, ed. Ernst Falzeder and Eva Brabant, translated by Peter T. Hoffer (Cambridge, MA: Harvard University Press, 2000), p. 248.
6. Weiss, *Sigmund Freud as a Consultant*, pp. 53-54.
7. *Letters of Sigmund Freud 1873-1939*, ed. Ernst. L. Freud (London: The Hogarth Press, 1961), p. 366.

8. Theodor Reik, *Ritual: Four Psychoanalytic Studies*, translated by Douglas Bryan (New York: Grove Press, 1946).
9. Eran J. Rolnik, "Between Ideology and Identity: Psychoanalysis in Jewish Palestine (1918-1948)," *Psychoanalysis and History*, Vol. 4, No. 2 (Summer 2002), pp. 216-17. See also Paul Roazen, *Freud: Political and Social Thought* (New York: Alfred A. Knopf, 1968; third edition, with new introduction; New Brunswick, NJ: Transaction Publishers, 1999), pp. 167-192.
10. For an interesting exploration of Freud's relation to Christianity, see Paul C. Vitz, *Sigmund Freud's Christian Unconscious* (New York: The Guilford Press, 1988).
11. *Letters of Sigmund Freud 1873-1939*, ed. Ernst L. Freud, p. 366.
12. Ernest Jones, *Sigmund Freud: Life and Work*, Vol. 1 (New York: Basic Books, 1957), p. 360.
13. John C. Burnham, *Jelliffe: American Psychoanalyst and Physician, and His Correspondence with Sigmund Freud and C. G. Jung*, ed. William McGuire (Chicago, University of Chicago, Press, 1983), pp. 240-45.
14. Contrast, for example, Freud's letters to William Bayard Hale about his study of Woodrow Wilson with Freud's comments to Theodor Reik about Hale: see Edwin A. Weinstein, "Bullitt, Freud, and Woodrow Wilson," *Journal of the American Academy of Psychoanalysis*, Vol. 16, No. 3 (1988), p. 352-53, and Theodor Reik, *Listening With the Third Ear* (New York: Farrar, Straus, and Co., 1948), pp. 120.
15. Masud Khan to Anna Freud, July 7, 1970, op. cit.
16. See Paul Roazen, *Brother Animal: The Story of Freud and Tausk* (New Brunswick, NJ: Transaction Publishers, 1990), pp. 134-41; "Sandor Ferenczi," *Standard Edition*, Vol. 22 (London: Hogarth Press, 1953-74), pp. 227-29 and *The Complete Correspondence of Sigmund Freud and Ernest Jones, 1908-1939*, ed. R. Andrew Paskauskas (Cambridge, MA: Harvard University Press, 1993), p. 721; "Dr. Ernest Jones," *Standard Edition*, Vol. 21, pp. 249-50 and Young Bruehl, *Anna Freud*, op. cit., p. 178.
17. Weiss, *Sigmund Freud as a Consultant*, pp. 56-57.
18. Ibid., p. 55.
19. Quoted in Benvenuto, "A Glimpse of Psychoanalysis in Italy," op. cit., p. 44.
20. *International Journal of Psychoanalysis*, Vol. 17 (1937), p. 96.
21. Weiss, *Sigmund Freud as a Consultant*, pp. 57-58.
22. "Eissler Interview," op. cit., p. 34.
23. Weiss, *Sigmund Freud as a Consultant*, p. 36.
24. Ibid., p. 51.
25. *The Complete Correspondence of Sigmund Freud and Karl Abraham* (London: Karmac, 2002), p. 94.
26. Denis Mack Smith, *Modern Italy: A Political History* (Ann Arbor: University of Michigan Press, 1997), p. 64.
27. Weiss, *Sigmund Freud as a Consultant*, op. cit., pp. 58-59.

28. Ibid., p. 64.
29. "On the History of the Psychoanalytic Movement," *Standard Edition*, Vol. 14, p. 32.
30. "Introduction to Edoardo Weiss's *Elements of Psychoanalysis*," *Standard Edition*, Vol. 21, p. 256.
31. Weiss, *Sigmund Freud as a Consultant*, p. 69.
32. See for example Paul Roazen, "Using Oral History About Freud: A Case in His 'Secret Essay,'" *American Imago*, Vol. 58, No. 4 (Winter 2001), pp. 793-812. See also Roazen, *On The Freud Watch: Public Memoirs* (London: Free Association Books, 2003), ch. 12, pp. 174-189.
33. Weiss, *Sigmund Freud as a Consultant*, pp. 70-71.
34. Ibid., p. 75; Denis Mack Smith, *Modern Italy: A Political History*, p. 363.
35. Weiss, *Sigmund Freud as a Consultant*, p. 81.
36. *The Correspondence of Sigmund Freud and Sandor Ferenczi*, Vol. 3, p. 422.
37. Weiss, *Sigmund Freud as a Consultant*, p. 82.

10

Tolerance and Loyalty

Any attempt on my part to try to communicate what I learned from Weiss is inevitably bound to make the process more linear and clear cut than the experience actually was; even now new thoughts still come to me. During the interviews we kept coming back to his letters from Freud, since that was the concrete historical evidence on which he could expertly expand. I was picking up new ideas and altered perspectives as we went along, and Weiss, too, told me that as we talked new memories came back to him. We got to understand each other's ways of communicating, and I think we both ended up liking the exchanges. He loaned me more technical papers of his to read; I also continued to tackle his books, and this understanding of his work was an essential constituent of our ability to get on. After I first saw him in April 1965 for the first couple of sessions, there was that period in May when I saw him for seven more meetings. In June 1966, I once again went back to see him in Chicago, at a time when my own research was more advanced; then I saw him twice for a total of about eight more hours. We stayed in touch by mail up until Weiss's death in December 1970.

One of my interviewing techniques with Weiss was to read him the names of members of the Italian Psychoanalytic Society from the 1930s. (I did the same in Britain with Edward Glover, and also with Kata Levy for the Hungarian analytic group.) My reading from that old roster did seem to help remind Weiss how difficult a time analysis had had in those days. It was not then popular in Italy, and the old-fashioned psychiatrists could score easy points against Freud. Morselli was only one such "bad character" who Weiss remembered. In France too the reception of psychoanalysis was held back on the grounds that Freud was part of an alien German influence; this aloofness was partially made possible by the excellence of the natively French neurological tradition.

Within Italy, Weiss felt he had had two staunch supporters in Rome, both of whom came to him on the basis of the book of lectures that he published with Freud's Preface: Servadio and Perrotti. Weiss subsequently analyzed them both, and arranged for them to become, like himself, members of the Vienna Psychoanalytic Society. (The Italian Society was not then accepted as a part of the IPA.) Although both Servadio and Perrotti had not gotten on well, I did not inquire enough into the nature of their quarrels. In addition to these two star pupils of Weiss's, analysis in Italy was notably helped by the cooperation of the Princess Lampedusa, whose husband wrote that great novel *The Leopard*. I had never had occasion to read it before Weiss told me how "beautiful" it was. Weiss did think that what the Princess wrote psychoanalytically was "nonsense," and for a time she became president of the Italian Psychoanalytic Society after World War II, but for the sake of the movement Weiss thought it had "helped to have a Princess." The only other princess in Freud's cause was Marie Bonaparte in Paris.

Inevitably issues came up that Weiss felt unsure about talking to me about. Rudolf Reitler, for example, had been among the earliest of Freud's followers in Vienna. The first beginnings of the Vienna Psychoanalytic Society came in the autumn of 1902, after Freud first got his titular, adjunct professorial appointment, making him an "extraordinarius" as opposed to getting a regular faculty title. Freud wrote a postcard to four men suggesting that they meet at his home to discuss his work. Rudolf Reitler, Alfred Adler, Max Kahane, and Wilhelm Stekel were the ones so invited. Weiss hesitated before telling me that Reitler, an analyst "from the first time," had contracted syphilitic general paresis. Weiss said he had sent Reitler some patients (Reitler did not use the couch), and that it was from them that he first heard of Reitler's mental disturbances. (For all the intensive training analysts get, after they are qualified they are on their own without supervision. In 1942 Clarence P. Oberndorf, personally unhappy about how he had fared with Freud in Vienna, suggested that it become a custom that "if a case has been under classic psychoanalytic treatment, four to five hours a week, for more than 300 hours, it be reviewed by another analyst, or preferably a panel of three analysts."[1] This suggestion of Oberndorf's has never been taken up.) Tausk had told Weiss that Reitler's comments at the Vienna Society confirmed the diagnosis; Reitler's speech had grown disordered. (Max Kahane also came to a bad end, although by then he no longer was coming to the Society; he committed suicide in 1923.[2] Stekel too, already seriously diabetic, died by his own hand in London just after the outbreak of World War II.[3])

Although Weiss remained a member of the Vienna Society until its formal dissolution under the Nazis in 1938, he rarely went to any meetings. He often saw Freud on trips to Vienna once or twice annually, but this was mainly for the sake of consultations about patients. But Weiss still knew the early Vienna group from the time he had been there before World War I. He remembered having sent many patients to Sadger, who had "a special interest" in treating homosexuals. Weiss did not consider him a very good analyst, but he was a senior member of Freud's group, even older than Federn; Sadger was Wilhelm Reich's first analyst. (Afterwards Reich went to both Federn and Sandor Rado.) Weiss knew that in London, England, Sadger had written a manuscript critical of Freud, but that "they" (presumably mainly Jones) would not let him publish it and the book was destroyed; then Sadger had gone "into oblivion" and "people did not mention him." Maxim Steiner was another early member of Freud's group in Vienna, a urologist who did not analyze much; Freud sent him patients who were impotent, for example, to check them for organic problems. Steiner remained a urologist, and Weiss thought he was a good one.

Among the early analysts we talked about, Ludwig Jekels, a Pole, came up as "the oldest but not too brilliant"; others spoke more highly of Jekels, for example Helene Deutsch, also Polish, and I suspect that Weiss's evaluation was partly a colored one since he singled Jekels out for having been critical of Federn's ego psychology. Weiss thought that Herbert Silberer, though, was " a very intelligent man" who killed himself in 1923.[4] Silberer's achievement was to interpret symbols in a different way than Freud.[5] Silberer was "rather close" to Jung's approach, and therefore not "in good harmony" with the others in the Vienna group; little by little "he drifted away." The feeling in the Vienna Society was that someone in a "family" should not become disloyal, and both Weiss, who had seven siblings and Wanda with eight brothers and sisters of her own, had come from huge families. Freud himself had five sisters and a brother, besides two half-brothers who had moved to England while he was a small child.

Weiss was shocked when I read him Freud's two-line letter to Silberer nine months before his death: "I request that you do not make the intended visit with me. As the result of observation and impressions of recent years I no longer desire personal contact with you."[6] Although these words have been in the literature now for over thirty years, since I first put them there having come across them unused in Jones's files in London, I have rarely ever seen them commented on or even cited.

As for other pioneering analysts, Weiss said he had once been in Alfred Adler's house in Vienna. Weiss still could use the stereotypical label "superficial" to describe Adler's thinking. He struck Weiss as a "simple" but "persuasive" man. When Weiss questioned him as to whether he did not think he was too "one-sided," which was the standard Freudian reproach of Adler, he had denied it. Like Adler, Sandor Ferenczi had also ended up on bad terms with Freud; Ferenczi had often come from Budapest to Vienna for pre-World War I meetings with Freud's group. Weiss thought Ferenczi was both exceptionally original and intelligent, although Weiss "heard" that he had become unorthodox with patients. Weiss quietly laughed at his own metaphor when he described how Ferenczi had first "confessed" his errors to Freud and then gotten "absolution."

Freud himself had a complicated attitude toward Rome that no doubt was bound up with his general orientation toward the Catholic Church; it took what Freud regarded as an overcoming of a personal inhibition before he actually could visit there. "Frank" had had a special yearning for Rome too. After visiting there, Freud loved going back to Rome. Freud once told Weiss that he was so much enchanted with the city that when he retired he wanted to establish himself there; Freud appreciated the sculpture (more than the paintings) and the archeological sites. But Freud's plans about Rome were never to be realized. (Freud disliked Naples because of the poverty, although Weiss tried to "talk him out of it"; Freud did of course enjoy Capri and Pompeii.)

In Rome, Weiss thought, having moved there from Trieste in 1931, that he had started to have his own ideas; up until then he had "remained orthodox for a very long time." That analyst of the Jungian school named Ernst Bernhard had come to Rome, and Weiss found that many of his ideas were sound; his wife Wanda having gone to him for treatment proved decisive. To Weiss, "analysis should not be a church." Weiss knew that Federn had also had some original thoughts of his own, as later did Franz Alexander too. (Weiss literally sucked in his breath at how "orthodox" someone like Nunberg was; he was "more so" even than Otto Fenichel, since Nunberg even believed in Freud's concept of the death instinct. For years Fenichel's big textbook[7] was such a bible for orthodoxy that a skeptic like Rado once said it was a compendium of all the errors in psychoanalysis; Helene Deutsch also referred to Fenichel's obsessional sort of approach as the "cancer" of psychoanalysis. Yet Fenichel's reputation has been flourishing lately, as young scholars find a rich feast even in tortured intellectuality.[8])

Weiss knew more than most of what had happened to psychoanalysis in England, and that Jones had been especially "protective" of Melanie Klein. It was even thought in the 1930s that there was a danger of another great split in the analytic movement, with Britain becoming heretical; guest lecturers were exchanged between London and Vienna, in an effort to mediate between the forces of Klein and Jones as opposed to Anna Freud. Then, once Freud and his Viennese entourage arrived in London in 1938, Jones had to help avoid a break-up of the Society, or so Weiss said he had been told. Weiss was bitter about Jones on several accounts. He first met him at pre-World War I meetings of the Vienna Psychoanalytic Society, at a time when Jones was unhappily involved with a woman he later separated from; in those days Hanns Sachs would try to translate to Jones what was being said. Then, when Weiss threw a party for Jones on the occasion of his visit to Rome around 1934, Jones had said to Weiss that Freud only understood the dynamics of hysteria, and not the other neuroses. To Weiss this meant that Jones was almost unthinkably disloyal to Freud. In print, Weiss wrote, "Jones told me he agreed with Freud's psychodynamic formulation of hysteria, but disagreed with Freud's formulations of the obsessional and depressive neuroses."[9]

In talking to Weiss, I had learned something special about Freud's "intolerance," and why it could be so hard to disagree with him. It was not so much that Freud legislated against potential deviants, although he was capable of doing that, but rather that Freud could seduce by the force of his personality and the power of his mind. When I once directly asked whether Freud had been "seductive," Weiss hesitated for a moment since he thought that the question might imply a hostile appraisal of Freud's influence; but then he heartily agreed that Freud did succeed in seducing his followers. When Freud's students left his presence, they could find it easier to disagree. Even then it was difficult, since he remained a "psychic presence," to use one of Weiss's favorite notions. Like so many other analysts, including probably Freud himself, concepts for Weiss seemed to acquire an independent life of their own. Geography could be critical in emancipation. Weiss in Vienna was a complete believer, and he remained pretty much so even in Trieste; but in Rome Weiss could begin to find his own more independent way, although Weiss never felt tempted to swing as far as others had done in order to make up for their earlier servilities.

On the issue of geography, and how distance could be tempting to commit psychoanalytic heresy, I also asked: *Why did Freud dislike America so*? It would be hard to say, except that Freud did not "approve" of the level of alcoholism there. Freud seems to have disliked his American patients even though he had analyzed so many of them. I once cited to Weiss a story of Max Schur's about Freud's having complained about his American patients: "This race is sentenced to disappear from the face of the earth. They can no longer open their mouths to speak; soon they will also not be able to do so to eat, and they will die of starvation." Weiss immediately understood this complaint as a subjective confession on Freud's part, since it was he whose cancer was threatening him with starvation. "So," Weiss commented, "he projected!" [10] The intensity of Freud's feelings about America have never been rationally explicable, as they went beyond what could have been reasonably expected of other cultured Central Europeans.

What sorts of people did he think Freud would be especially good with? Weiss's answer was a story he had heard from his older sister Amalia. During her analysis Freud had said, at a point where she was hesitant and ashamed, that an analytic patient needs three qualities —the first is courage, the second is courage, and the third is courage. Weiss thought Freud had gotten this saying from a variation on one of Napoleon's aphorisms; in order to win a war one requires three things —money, money, and money. The inheritor of the French Revolution remained a hero to Central European Jews, who benefited from Napoleonic reforms putting an end to the ghettoes. (Danton had earlier said that what was needed in warfare was audacity, audacity, and audacity.) Weiss consistently maintained that in Freud's clinical practice signs of courage, truthfulness, and adherence to his teachings effected strong positive feelings in him.

When I knew Weiss his health was already uncertain; he had had a kidney removed in 1965, and ultimately died of uremic poisoning. In the mid-1960s, he had to take nitroglycerin for heart pain that could wake him up in the middle of the night. He had a pacemaker put in later. And his eyes had been operated on, which is why he often used a magnifying glass in order to read manuscripts and papers. But he never seemed to tire in my interviews, though he could repeat himself from time to time.

Through me, he sent word to Helene Deutsch about a former patient of his, the wife of a Chicago analyst that she too had seen once or twice; the woman was very satisfied with both Weiss and Helene Deutsch, although he thought her husband needed the help more. He was subtle enough to be able to do this without compromising the patient's identity. She followed what he had intended to communicate through me, who thereby became an innocent intermediary; it seems to me an example of just how exquisite both their Old World manners could be.

Weiss knew that I was planning to visit Anna Freud in the summer of 1965, for I had told him about it; but he said that he did not want me to mention him to her at all, although I suspected that he clearly wanted to hear what she spoke of him and psychoanalysis in Italy. A student of his there had earlier verified for him her dislike and disapproval of him. It had all started, he claimed, at an international congress of analysts in 1953, or perhaps as early as 1946 or 1947, when Anna kept avoiding any of his attempts to approach her. Weiss was still so unguarded that he never seemed to realize, even in 1965, that whatever he had said in interviews with Eissler in 1952 would have immediately been communicated to Anna. Once I saw her, and Weiss's name came up, she pronounced it with biting distaste, although she readily acknowledged that Trieste represented a special chapter in the history of psychoanalysis, a point that it took me years fully to appreciate for myself.

When I saw Weiss afterwards, one of the first things he wanted to know about was Anna's attitude toward him. She somehow had acted as if he had deserted "the cause." He remained worried that he would stand out in her mind as one of the "few" I had seen, and therefore was relieved to hear that I had also spoken with Heinz Hartmann, since he was then such a representative leader of orthodoxy. "What more can she do to me?" he plaintively asked at one point. On the one hand he tried to believe that he simply did not care anymore about her attitude toward him; at the same time he had assured me before I saw her: "If she says anything too disastrous, do not believe!" The more I knew him the more his idiosyncrasies in English seemed touching to me.

Weiss remained convinced that his problem with Anna lay with his wife having gone to Bernhard, that Jungian in Rome; and also, to repeat, Wanda had had some analytic sessions with Margarete Ruben, who later went to be with Anna in London and whom Weiss thought—perhaps mistakenly—carried malicious tales about Weiss's own contact with Bernhard. Weiss said she was Jewish, analyzed by Felix Boehm in Germany, but came to Italy after the Nazis rose to power; Weiss cited Fenichel about her having been ambitious and critical, and was deeply offended by her having diagnosed Federn's writings as "schizophrenic." As for Bernhard, Weiss said that he had merely "wanted to understand his position." To Weiss, Anna was "not interested in the truth," although at the same time he stuck to a faith in her fundamental "decency." Weiss was too personally hurt by Anna to appreciate how I think she had to mind any people who had secure ties to her father that did not go through her. In the years since her death in 1982 her power base in Britain has so evaporated that now her reputation and contributions may be in danger of getting lost.

The more Weiss had talked about Freud and the history of psychoanalysis, the clearer it became that Federn was for Weiss an alternative leader. Weiss seemed to me so devoted to Federn's memory that others, members of the Federn study group in New York for example, could often be more articulate about Federn's contribution than Weiss himself. As Weiss put it at one point, he had established a father transference to Freud, and a mother transference to Federn. While Freud remained for Weiss the great researcher, it was clear that as a therapist Weiss found Federn a kindlier figure to ally himself with.

Although Weiss did not make a great point of the matter, he admired the way Federn, although he considered marriage very important, fundamentally thought that a man's sexual life was a private question. That way the commitment of marital life was less likely to be threatening, a kind of castration. Although Freud had lacked an analyst of his own, Weiss cited Freud's having maintained that "as a safeguard, the analyst himself should have a satisfactory love life, in order to deal with the strong transference feelings of his patients."[11] Federn himself was also old fashioned enough to believe that a woman should be a little flirtatious; but he got on terribly with a real career woman like Helene Deutsch. She reveled in examples of Federn's absent-mindedness, and Erikson told a famous example of one of Federn's public slips of the tongue.[12] And Federn enjoyed retelling how while Helene Deutsch once intended to say "I have already notified all you gentlemen," she slipped with her acquired German and instead said: "I have already put you at a disadvantage." Somehow Freud succeeded in encouraging sibling rivalry among his pupils and could talk against them to each other; he ruled partly through dividing and conquering.

Above all, Weiss liked the way Federn had cared so much for helping people. He was preeminently a healer, while Freud craved much more for scientific understanding. Politically, Federn was a Social Democrat, and as a therapist more optimistic than Freud; Federn was also more tolerant of the way people's egos could need support. Tausk had initiated the concepts of identity and of "ego boundaries" before Federn began using them; those ideas were designed to emphasize that psychological illness could arise from a weak or defensive ego, in need of being supported, rather than to trace it, as Freud did to an excess of instinctual strength.

Later theorists like Margaret Mahler appreciated what Federn had tried to do earlier. For Federn weak ego boundaries led to the tendencies to introject and to project. Schizophrenia was not caused, as Freud's thinking supposed, "by the withdrawal of object libido into the ego, but rather by a deficiency of ego libido"; depersonalization was due to a lack of ego cathexis rather than inadequate object cathexis.[13] Federn's thinking meant that it could be a mistake to arouse normal object love in a seriously disturbed patient, lest they get worse because of a lack of ego libido. Such people can withdraw from the world defensively, out of lack of emotional resources. Federn did not think that their problems meant that one could not approach therapeutically patients with deficits like that. Patients can be right about themselves and their therapists; as one of Weiss's patients told him, when assured that suicide was no danger, that if he killed himself all Weiss would do was change the diagnosis, and Weiss conceded to me the truth of that remark. In keeping with Federn's whole orientation, Weiss could write about trying to make "his psychotic patients repress some drives, in order to enhance the integrative capacity of their ego."[14]

Freud refused to go along with Federn's kind of reasoning; and Freud found Federn's phenomenological approach to the ego incomprehensible. Nonetheless, it was Federn who ended up taking out of Europe the multi-volume *Minutes* of the Vienna Psychoanalytic Society. Weiss thought that Federn approached the psychoses better, and more humanely than Freud. Federn's kindliness had taken the form of a stand in behalf of the psychotherapy of the most severely ill, and without the kind of massive confrontations recommended by some later thinkers.

Of psychotics Freud once notably wrote: "I do not care for these patients...they annoy me and...I find them alien to me and to everything human. A peculiar kind of intolerance which undoubtedly disqualifies me as psychiatrist."[15] Federn, and Weiss as well, were convinced that something hormonal or chemical lay behind the great mental collapses, and by now more and more evidence has accumulated about the genetic basis for psychosis; even today however much remains unknown, and the controversy about nature versus nurture, as well as the role of the environment in promoting mental illness, remains highly conjectural. Freud's own lack of interest in "immoral" people with an inadequate ego meant to Weiss that many "confessions" were made to Federn that nobody would have "dared" to give to Freud. Much as Weiss admired Federn, he knew that he was not the speaker that Freud was, although Federn did have the ambition to be able, like Anna Freud and her father, to lecture without notes. Freud himself had spoken like a book.

Before concluding my interviewing with Weiss, I harked back to my early interest in the national differences in the reception of Freud's ideas, and asked: *Were there any special "resistances," or cultural blocks to self-knowledge, among Italians*? Yes, the Italians did show much more attachment to the mother than would have been the case elsewhere. "Mother fixations" among Italian patients was more prominent than in America for example. (Erich Fromm gave me the same example about the patients he had seen in Mexico. Both countries are unusually family conscious. When one reads how "it is only with difficulty that Italians can conceive of themselves as solitary subjects,"[16] apart from families, it seems a mild instance of the Chinese today moving away from Confucianism.) And Weiss thought it was "certainly true" that Freud had underplayed the role of the mother. Few of Weiss's own patients in Italy were religious Catholics, unlike, Weiss said, the Irish; the Italian students were apt to be anti-religious, with songs against the Church, and also "very sexual." Weiss thought that the proportion of homosexual males in Italy was 4 percent, which he held to be "a universal figure" for all countries, although a little more than that were bisexual. Although the Italians were not as organically oriented in psychiatry as the Germans had been, Weiss emphasized that within intellectual circles in Italy during his time there psychoanalysis had been barely accepted. Yet I think that over a hundred years after Freud started out we are as afflicted with the bane of positivism as ever, even though a great philosopher-psychologist like William James, who approvingly read Freud in the 1890s, long ago struggled to keep the spiritual dimension in focus.

I cannot forget how at one point Weiss had gently protested in his own behalf: "It was all over fifty years ago!" And he also once tried to deflect my insistent curiosity by pointing out: "I was younger then than you are now!" He was trying to explain his difficulties sometimes in coming up with appropriate memories to answer all my inquiries. At times he could be dismayed, and incredulous, that I still had "more questions." I was fortunate in having that younger member of the Chicago Psychoanalytic Institute, aware of my work, who helped intervene with Weiss in my behalf to make sure he understood the historical importance of what I was aiming to reconstruct. Although Weiss had been retired as a training analyst at the Institute he still was trying to please.

When he once said to me "Do not be like Jones!" he meant that I should ask him beforehand about quoting from any of his Freud letters, or threatening the privacy of any former patients. Of course, I did not then know I would ever publish anything specifically about Weiss; at the time nothing of mine was then in print. But he suspected, with all my note taking, that perhaps something might come of it eventually. At one point he wondered "why" otherwise I continued to write so much down; that was both a question as well as an exclamation. Both of us were relieved as I finished my set of interviews; as he observed, benevolently and yet with a quietly amazed sort of irritation: "you had a million questions."

Notes

1. C. P. Oberndorf, "Failures with Psychoanalytic Therapy," in *Failures in Psychiatric Treatment*, ed. Paul H. Hoch (New York: Grune and Stratton, 1948), p. 19.
2. Paul Roazen, *Helene Deutsch: A Psychoanalyst's Life* (New Brunswick, NJ: Transaction Publishers, 1992), p. 209.
3. Paul Roazen, *Freud and His Followers* (New York: Alfred A. Knopf, 1974), p. 222.
4. Ibid., pp. 338-41.
5. Martin Bergmann, "The Place of Paul Federn's Ego Psychology in Psychoanalytic Metapsychology,"*Journal of the American Psychoanalytic Association*, Vol. 11, No. 1 (Jan. 1963), pp. 105-6.
6. Paul Roazen, *Brother Animal: The Story of Freud and Tausk* (New Brunswick, NJ: Transaction Publishers, 1990), pp. 157.
7. Otto Fenichel, *The Psychoanalytic Theory of Neurosis* (New York: W. W. Norton, 1945).
8. Russell Jacoby, *The Repression of Psychoanalysis: Otto Fenichel and the Political Freudians* (New York: Basic Books, 1983); Johannes Reichmayr and Elke Mühlleitner, editors, *Otto Fenichel 119 Rundbrief*, 2 volumes (Frankfurt, Stroemfeld, 1998).
9. Edoardo Weiss, *Sigmund Freud as a Consultant: Recollections of a Pioneer in Psychoanalysis*, with an introduction by Martin Grotjahn (New York: Intercontinental Medical Book Corporation, 1970; New Brunswick, NJ: Transaction Publishers, 1991), p. 14.
10. Letter of Max Schur to Ernest Jones, Sept. 30, 1955 (Jones Archives). See also Roazen, *Freud: Political and Social Thought*, op. cit., pp. 315-16.
11. Weiss, *Sigmund Freud as a Consultant*, p. 40.
12. Roazen, *Freud and His Followers*, p. 331.
13. Bergmann, "The Place of Paul Federn's Ego Psychology in Psychoanalytic Metapsychology," p. 103.
14. Weiss, *Sigmund Freud as a Consultant*, p. 40.
15. Quoted in Ernst Federn, "Thirty-Five Years with Freud: In Honour of the 100th Anniversary of Paul Federn," *Journal of Clinical Psychology*, Monograph Supplement No. 32 (January 1972), p. 32.
16. Sergio Benvenuto, "A Glimpse at Psychoanalysis in Italy," *Journal of European Psychoanalysis*, No. 5 (Spring-Fall 1997), p. 39.

Afterwards

Following World War II, the Italian Psychoanalytic Society was reestablished, and the First Italian Psychoanalytic Congress was held in Rome on October 22-23, 1946. The Society had finally been accorded tentative recognition by the Central Executive of the International Psychoanalytic Association. Six former members of the Society were present: the Princess Lampedusa of Palma, Dr. Merloni, Professor Musatti, Dr. Perrotti, and Professor Servadio. Two additional new members were elected, and two candidates were under consideration for membership. A quarterly became the official organ of the Society. Perrotti was elected president, while honorary membership was conferred on Weiss.

The opening session took place in the large demonstration room of the Rome University Medical Clinic. According to the official report, submitted by Servadio, "For the first time after a long uphill fight psychoanalysis was receiving full acknowledgment by politicians and scientists in official positions. This was a further proof of progress and of the repudiation of Fascist ideas by the Italian nation."[1] Members of the government attended, and both the president of the Italian Republic and the prime minister sent their greetings. Besides the many professional papers that got delivered, telegrams also came in from Anna Freud in London and Weiss in Chicago. Italian Radio broadcast an interview with Perrotti and Sevadio on October 22, and on the October 25 a discussion on psychoanalysis by the Princess Lampedusa, along with four other analysts, was also carried on radio. Organized psychoanalysis in Italy was off to its postwar start.

How written history gets constructed has to remain a different story. Although the past deserves to be reconstructed for its own sake, too often Whig history prevails; that is, historical accounts are remembered for the sake of celebrating success, and providing an ancestry that makes people today feel good about themselves.

Yet I remain convinced that the importance of studying the past consists in precisely how it enables us to establish distance from the present.[2] History teaches the most when it gives us new perspectives on the present, telling us what we might not otherwise know or be inclined to want to hear. And therefore it is necessary, I think, to search for past figures who are on the whole forgotten or neglected.[3] Stories should not be told for the sake of convincing us about the seamlessness of the continuities from past to the present, with ourselves sitting pretty as the inheritors of progressive tendencies. History at its best challenges us to rethink what we believe to be true today. The world of old Trieste may be in some sense irrevocably lost now, but still be worth paying attention to for that very reason.

Now Weiss and I had spent a good deal of time talking about Weiss's old friend and medical classmate Victor Tausk, since I then had, with Helene Deutsch's help and encouragement, a special interest in research on this early psychoanalyst; Weiss later wrote a small separate piece about his reminiscences of Tausk, and made some key references to Tausk in his essay "My Recollections of Sigmund Freud" that introduced the collection of his Freud letters.

I do not want to burden this book about Weiss with too much further material on Tausk, except to say that at the time I was gathering this interviewing I knew so little about Trieste that I did not realize how Tausk, who was born in Slovakia and soon taken to Croatia, not only came from the same Hapsburg Empire as Weiss but from an area readily comprehensible to someone from Trieste, so close to the Balkans. Weiss's wife Wanda was, like Tausk, also Croatian. Although Tausk's father had worked in Bosnia, and Weiss's family was closer to Slovenia, a cultural basis existed for their friendship about which I remained ignorant not only at the time but for years thereafter. Of course, Vienna was the alluring intellectual capital for them all, and Tausk like Weiss was originally Jewish, but the specifics of Weiss's biography does newly illuminate for me the basis for how he could get on with Tausk.

My last two interviews with Weiss concentrated on what I had been learning then about Tausk, then a figure even more disturbingly ignored than Weiss now. At least in Italy today there is a need to pay attention to Weiss for the sake of filling in the ancestry for the growingly successful psychoanalytic movement there. Partly I was at the time using Weiss as a sounding board for what I was unearthing then about Tausk. Tausk however was a suicide, and therefore a skeleton in the psychoanalytic family closet. Weiss told me whatever he thought he knew about Tausk's character and unfortunate end. Tausk had been not only sympathetic to the treatment and understanding of the psychoses, but Tausk had originated the idea of ego boundaries. One sentence in Weiss's published account of his Freud impressions reflected Federn's thinking in a letter of his to his wife following Tausk's death that I showed Weiss: "gradually," Weiss too said of Freud, "he lost some of his compassion...when after the first World war Viktor Tausk was destitute and had fallen into a deep depression, Freud could not give his old friend the moral support he badly needed."[4] Although Weiss had been one of the first to alert me to the changes in Freud's writings once he knew he was dying of cancer, I had my own serious doubts about the way Federn, and subsequently Weiss, viewed Freud's role in Tausk's death. But Khan and Anna Freud clearly had the Tausk story in their minds when they were privately reacting to the prospect of publishing the Freud-Weiss letters.

Although psychiatry itself has, at least in North America, been moving in a different direction from what was the case when I knew Weiss, I am still impressed with the thematic similarities that still exist. The whole problem of the mind and its relation to the body, and the psychosomatic research Weiss pioneered in still remains an enduring dilemma. It is true that new technologies, in the form of fresh drugs, have been invented; and, more or less the way Freud had anticipated would be the case, old-fashioned psychoanalytic understanding can no longer be pursued in the same way it once was. Quicker solutions to human troubles are at hand, and no doubt even more are on the horizon.

But dogmatism in the human sciences remains a permanent feature of intellectual life. The example of a life and career like that of Weiss has, I think, something critical to teach. He reported to me, for example, how Freud had once maintained that there had been so many fights and splits within psychoanalysis because of the different degrees of evidence that are available in this field. Uncertainty promotes ideological thinking, and when it comes to understanding and helping human suffering there are bound to be permanent philosophic dilemmas. Controversies should exist when so much of what is at issue concerns rival conceptions of how life ought to be lived. As long as the Socratic objective of living an examined existence remains a central value, heated disagreements are going to continue. Even the discovery of the existence of neurotransmitters does not eliminate the need to evaluate the goals of being human, and what the good life consists in. However single-minded Freud can sound in forwarding his cause, nowadays drug companies, earning billions of dollars every year, deserve the closest kind of scrutiny.[5]

Authoritarianism in clinical thinking and practice remains as much a problem as ever. Of course scientific knowledge advances, and technological progress ensures that new instruments for healing will be available; but how these changes are implemented, and the spirit in which such work proceeds, remains an open question. Power still corrupts, and absolute power remains as absolutely dangerous as ever. People remain self-deceiving, and even if Freud could mislead himself about his own best achievements, others too are capable of different varieties of self-deception. Studying the past should not be for the sake of imitating anything specific, but for the purpose of enlarging our imaginative capacities. Tolerance and charity arise from an educated consciousness, and there fortunately seems no end to what we need to learn.

Notes

1. *International Journal of Psychoanalysis*, Vol. 27 (1946), p. 171.
2. Paul Roazen, "The Importance of the Past," in *On the Freud Watch: Public Memoirs* (London: Free Association Books, 2003), ch. 1, pp. 13-26.
3. Paul Roazen, *The Historiography of Psychoanalysis* (New Brunswick, NJ: Transaction Publishers, 2000), part 5, pp. 193-227.
4. Edoardo Weiss, *Sigmund Freud as a Consultant: Recollections of a Pioneer in Psychoanalysis*, with an introduction by Martin Grotjahn (New York: Intercontinental Medical Book Corporation, 1970; New Brunswick, NJ: Transaction Publishers, 1991), p. 8. Compare with Federn in *Brother Animal*, pp. 153-54.
5. David Healy, *The Creation of Psychopharmacology* (Cambridge, MA: Harvard University Press, 2002), David Healy, *The Anti-Depressant Era* (Cambridge, MA: Harvard University Press, 1997), and David Healy, "Conflicting Interests in Toronto," *Perspectives in Biology and Medicine*, Vol. 45, No. 2 (Spring 2002), pp. 250-63.

Acknowledgements

In addition to my citations earlier in the various Notes, I remain grateful to the following people who have talked or written to me about Weiss's career in Italy and the U.S.: Dr. Jacqueline Amati-Mehler, Dr. James Anderson, Dr. Jerome Beigler, Dr. Helen Beiser, Sergio Benvenuto, Dr. Martin Bergmann, Dr. Carlo Bonomi, Dr. Sonia Buglione, Henry Cohen, Dr. Peter Giovacchini, Dr. Bertram J. Cohler, Dr. Daria Colombo, Dr. Richard Cook, Dr. Arthur Couch, Dr. Aaron Esman, Dr. Ernst Falzeder, Dr. Sylvia Flescher, Prof. Larry J. Friedman, Dr. John Gedo, Dr. Renee Gelman, Verne Horne, Christian Huber, Dr. Jerome Kavka, Dr. Oliver Kerner, Professor Don Levine, Dr. E. James Lieberman, Miriam Meyerhof, Dr. Alain de Mijolla, Glen Miller, Michael Molnar, Dr. George Moraitis, Dr. Paul Ornstein, Dr. George Pollock, Dr. Joseph Reppen, Dr. Arthur Reinitz, Dr. Eran Rolnik, A. P. Sidhar, Dr. Roberto Speziale-Bagliacca, Riccardo Steiner, Barbara Weiss, Guido and Barbara Weiss, Emilio and Hilda Weiss, and Marianna Weiss. Dr. Jack Drescher helped me understand various pieces of the relevant Italian literature. At the Library of Congress both Fred Bauman and Marvin Kranz have facilitated my work there. I have often relied on Vivian Goldman's help at the Boston Psychoanalytic Institute's library, and none of my work could proceed without the assistance of Harvard University's Widener Library.

Photo Credits

Photographs of the Weiss family, courtesy of Guido Weiss.
Edoardo Weiss, drawing by Olga Szekely-Kovacs, photograph courtesy of Judith Dupont.
Trieste, photograph courtesy of Peter Hartshorn.
Italo Svevo and his wife and daughter, photograph courtesy of Letizia Svevo Fonda Savio.
Paul Federn, photograph courtesy of Guido Weiss.
Concetta Forzano, photograph courtesy of Guido Weiss.
IPA Lucerne Conference, 1934, photographs courtesy of Tim Gidal.

Index

0 1341 1431409 6